Setting Goals

by

John Renesch

Why should we just take what we get,
when we can choose exactly what we want?

— John Renesch

TABLE OF CONTENTS

DEDICATION

To individual courage, character and conviction as exemplified by those individuals (those who are mentioned herein as well as those who are not) who looked at how they really wanted their lives to be.

PREFACE

The purpose of this book is to assist you in obtaining absolute clarity on what you want in every area of your life. If you are willing to get clearer about your intentions in life, if you are willing to get more value out of your life, if you are interested in improving the quality of your day-to-day experiences, then you can look forward to taking the first step toward a richer, fuller, more satisfying life.

This book does not suggest purposes for your life. It does not suggest goals either. This book is designed to be a tool for you to determine and clarify all of your own desires, your own wants, your own dreams, looking at them, establishing your willingness to have them in your life, and making them even more real by writing them down. You may discover many desires about which you were previously unaware.

I strongly recommend that you read this book in *as short a time span as you can arrange in your schedule.* An absolute essential for getting value from this book is doing the exercises in Chapter IX (actually listing what you want) in *one continuous sitting.* I'd like to see you read the book in a relatively short time period, such as one day or a weekend, depending on your reading ability, speed, and comprehension. I personally believe that shorter period of time in which you can absorb the material contained in this book, the more value you are likely to receive from it.

Remember, the time you give to yourself in order to get clear about what you want could be the most valuable gift you ever give yourself.

There is more value in giving yourself a day or two on the subject of what you want in your life than you could possibly receive by doing anything else! Think about it. What else could you do that could be more important than to resolve what you want in life— ALL OF IT!

In order to achieve the maximum degree of value from this book, you must be willing to *have* the things you *say* you want and recognize that this may be a significant change in your lifestyle; you must be willing to create an environment for really looking at what you want, taking responsibility for getting value from the entire experience.

Welcome to a level of personal responsibility that few people ever reach. Congratulations for coming this far.

John Renesch

Published by Context Publications
20 Lomita Avenue
San Francisco, CA 94122
(415) 664-4477
ISBN: 0-932654-08-8

Action may not always bring happiness, but there is no happiness without action.

Disraeli

CHAPTER I

WHAT WE ALL WANT

There is an anecdote that I recall reading some time ago about a young boy trudging along a country road with a small calibre rifle over his shoulder. A man walking in the opposite direction asks the youngster what kind of creature he is hunting. The boy replies, "Dunno, sir, I ain't seen it yet."

The boy's reply is a perfect example of how most people run their lives—they are out to accomplish, attain, and achieve, but they aren't sure what!

Imagine going shopping for a new automobile without any idea of what kind of car you want to buy. Picture yourself walking through car lots, dealer showrooms, and checking through the want-ads in the papers, without any idea of what you want. Many people do shop for cars in this manner, by the way, so this example is not an uncommon analogy.

Conversely, imagine yourself knowing *exactly* what you want and doing the same thing, *but* knowing what you're looking for. Can you see the difference in how you will feel while seeking what you want, making the selection, and coming home with your new car?

Most people don't know what they want, but they're certain they don't have it. Every human being has been here sometime in his life and many people spend their entire lives "knowing they don't have it." Few people, however, take the time to look and see what "it" is.

It is my observation that most people spend more time planning a trip to the grocery store for one meal than they spend looking at what they want for themselves for their entire lifetime!

As human beings, we are all remarkably similar in our desires for ourselves. All of us have a different picture, or representation, or concept of what it looks like but we all seem to want that oftentimes elusive peak experience. It has been referred to as paradise, total fulfillment, oneness with the Divine, total success, and many other labels.

In a somewhat primitive culture, this experience may have come from catching a fresh three-pound fish for the evening meal; for a more civilized culture it may be represented by the successful landing of a spacecraft on Mars. For a high school athlete, this experience could be qualifying for the varsity basketball team. For a retired farmer in Kansas, it might be seeing a picture of his first grandson.

SATISFACTION

I call this experience "satisfaction"—a level above simple gratification (which is about attaining those things we feel we *must* have to survive). Satisfaction is a moving, kinetic experience. Accomplishing something you really want in your life can be an extremely valuable experience and the final act of achievement can be very exhilarating indeed!

The feeling that accompanies this sense of completion includes a real "rush." Your heartbeat quickens; you seem to radiate tremendous amounts of energy; you seem to be more alive than ever; you don't even have the capacity for a negative attitude or a pessimistic thought; you feel proud, self-realized, extremely healthy—happy!

Then, it disappears! It's over! That's it! Poof! What happened to it? After all that time (and perhaps, all that struggle and effort), where did all the good stuff go? There are only memories now and it seems all too quickly forgotten.

That experience that we label "being happy," that I call "satisfaction," is an alignment of many concurrent increments of feeling satisfied, all moving by us very rapidly, never to be experienced again. These moments are gone forever and you need to continually produce more of them to maintain the experience of feeling satisfied.

Visualize satisfaction as the feeling and attitude about yourself that you experience while moving closer to a predetermined end result, a goal. Also, imagine the feeling of contentment and completion upon attaining, accomplishing, or achieving that end result.

Satisfaction is not a state. It is a *passing* experience. It is the being, doing, or having of what you set out to attain, accomplish, or achieve.

I have a nickname for satisfaction—I call it the "-ingness" in life. It relates to the movement or progress itself rather than some static state.

As an example, recall a big problem that you resolved for yourself recently—one that you found a true solution for. Recall the feeling you had while you were providing the solution, carrying out the activities that, when added up to a total, made up the final result—*no more problem.* Do you see how the satisfaction came out of the *doing* or *providing* of the solution? There is certainly some joy in recalling *how* you solved the problem (I don't want to invalidate enjoyable memories). However, I want you to notice how it felt to solve the problem in terms of personal satisfaction. Once the problem disappears as a result of your solution, the "-ingness" is over with. It is now time for the next project.

Satisfaction *is not* the attainment of a desired condition. Satisfaction *is not* the achievement of a goal. Satisfaction *is not* the accomplishment of an end or the state of having reached a goal. Satisfaction *is* attitude in which we hold the act of attaining. It occurs during the act of achieving what we want, whether it takes place over one week, ten weeks, or ten years! Satisfaction is a fleeting moment, or a collection of many fleeting moments. There is no satisfaction being comfortable, sitting on some achievement.

Satisfaction is a totally personal experience—every person will experience it differently. However, some common factors in the degree to which you will experience satisfaction include the degree of difficulty in attaining the desired result, the number or frequency of the results produced, and the quality of the results you produce. The degree of personal responsibility you take for achieving the final result will also contribute to the degree of satisfaction you experience, along with the amount of time that transpires from the time the goal was set until the final accomplishment, the exactness with which you produce the result, the number of new abilities and capabilities you discover within yourself, and the amount of increased self-esteem you experience personally.

There is no ultimate place or plateau where "it" (ultimate satisfaction or ultimate happiness) is. There is no mountain where "it" hangs out. "It" exists in the act of climbing the mountain. And, there will always be another mountain (another goal). That's just the way it is. That's the way life works.

THE FIRST STEP

Satisfaction seldom exists where pure chance dictates what is happening in your life. It comes from determining what you want and seeing to it that it happens. It is a function of your participation in the results, taking personal responsibility for the way your life works out.

The first step toward satisfaction, therefore, is to determine what you really intend to do with your life—*where* you are going, *what* you want, *who* you want to be. The most effective method of determining these intentions, from my own experience, is by focusing or looking at each area of your life and examining it in detail—by focusing on one area of your life at a time. This is the principle I used in my all day seminars in the mid-1970s—Focusing Seminars.

To maximize the experience of satisfaction, it stands to reason that you need to be as clear as possible about what you want. Otherwise, how can you feel truly satisfied with the results? This is what I stressed in the seminars—exact as detailed a description as people could envision—the Focusing technique.

For example, Richard is refinishing and repainting his wooden motorboat. This activity requires a commitment of time and energy and could be either a chore or an exciting venture for Richard, depending upon the clarity and certainty he possesses about what result he wants.

If Richard isn't sure about the color he wants the boat to be, and he has compromised on his selection of paint, or, if he isn't sure if he is going to keep the boat or sell it after he paints it, the refinishing and repainting could be not only less than *very* satisfying, but indeed *unsatisfying* !

Conversely, if Richard was really clear about the color he wanted and what he was going to do with his refinished boat when he completed the project, the entire job could be an extremely satisfying adventure.

The Focusing technique allows us to become crystal clear about what we want in life by examining each area of our lives in detail, seeking out the things that we want that we don't have and noticing those things that we have that we don't want.

Through the Focusing technique, we can identify what we consider important in our lives—those things that we really want for ourselves, in our relationships and in how we live.

CLARITY

The satisfaction gained from the accomplishment of a goal will usually be in proportion to the clarity with which you set it. The more vague the objectives, the more uncertain will be the sense of fulfillment. The more clearly you've expressed the goal, the more satisfying will be the feeling that you experience with the achievement.

This feeling of satisfaction is normally associated with the many incremental accomplishments on the way to the final accomplishment—the goal. It is the nature of this sensation to disappear once the accomplishment has been realized. Then it's time for the next goal, and the next, and the next, and so on. Each accomplishment opens the door to an even higher goal level—presenting an opportunity to continually expand your ability and effectiveness. This is what satisfaction is all about and it is a real adventure!

OUR BASIC NEEDS

What motivates us as human beings? What is it that creates our desire to move, to react, to better the quality of our lives? The late Dr. Abraham H. Maslow, a pioneer in humanistic psychology, authored a multilevel description of the priorities of man's basic needs as he observed them. He called this description the Hierarchy of Needs. They are:

● The Physiological Needs—feelings of physical sating and glut; food, sex, and sleep.

● The Safety Needs—the feelings of safety, peace, security, lack of danger and threat.

● The Belongingness and Love Needs—feelings of belongingness, of being one of a group, of identification with group goals and triumphs, of acceptance, or having a place of at-homeness. Feelings of loving and being loved, of being loveworthy, of love identification.

- The Esteem Needs—feelings of self-reliance, self-respect, self-esteem, confidence, trust in one's self; feelings of ability, achievement, success, ego-strength, respectworthiness, prestige, leadership, independence.

- The Need for Self-Actualization—the feelings of self-actualization, self-fulfillment, self-realization, of more and more complete development and fruition of one's resources and potentialities and consequent feelings of growth, maturity, health, and autonomy.

Once we are certain that our basic needs have been provided, once we know that we are going to physically survive the big bad wolf and the bogey-man, once we are convinced that our food, clothes, and shelter needs are fulfilled, for what purpose do we keep ourselves operational?

We know that we work! We have mastered that art of simple existing. We know that our primary survival needs have been taken care of. All our parts function properly and their maintenance seems assured. So, what is next?

What is our purpose to being functioning human beings? Why are we taking up space on this planet? Personally, all I can envision doing for *myself* is going out in the world to experience higher and higher degrees of satisfaction—coming closer and closer to my maximum potential, a totally unknown quantity. I find this to be tremendously satisfying!

THE TRAFFIC JAM PHILOSOPHY

While preparing material for this book, I was sitting in a traffic snarl-up in the Chinatown area of San Francisco. Suddenly it hit me! I discovered a vital principle sitting in the middle of Kearny Street! Who would have thought . . . ?

I had been giving considerable thought to all the material I was gathering and there seemed to be some element missing for me. Not being a psychologist, I had felt that I might be lacking in some knowledge of basic principles concerning human motivation. I did know, however, that I was getting extremely high and feeling terrifically satisfied whenever I was moving towards my own goals, and I didn't need to have a Ph.D. to know that it worked.

There, sitting in the traffic jam, I could see how it all fit into man's nature. I saw that I could state it unequivocally, from my own observation, that

IT IS MAN'S NATURE TO BE MOVING, PROGRESS-ING ON SOME COURSE, TO IMPROVE HIS POSI-TION OR CONDITION.

Sitting in the traffic jam, I watched how people reacted to being at a standstill in their cars. I observed the impatience, the tapping of fingers on roofs and steering wheels. I could see how drivers tended to inch forward every once in a while, even when there was no place to go. When they could not move any longer, I noticed how they looked. I watched the expressions on their faces. I could see how their breathing changed, how they shifted in their seats, with slouching or "relaxed" resignation. Some of them seemed angry. Some seemed frustrated. Most were resigned to boredom. Others were almost "unconscious." I noticed how the passengers were affected. Observe yourself in these circumstances and notice how *you* feel when you are being prevented from moving toward your destination and how differently you feel when you are on your way again.

Likewise, in our lives, when we become aware of having stopped in some aspect or area of our lives, we naturally want to get moving again. When we notice that things have become dull, less interesting and challenging, boring (or whatever labels we want to attach to these feelings), it seems like it's time to move on.

If we are being, doing, or having the very best where we are, then perhaps it's time to go on to something new. If things aren't at their very best, perhaps it's the time to perfect them and totally abolish the mediocrity in our lives.

Like the drivers sitting in their cars in the traffic jam, many people become resigned to the condition they are in, and don't do anything about it. They end up going deeper and deeper into unconsciousness instead of moving on. This unconsciousness covers up the dissatisfaction and helps them forget their frustration. Sometimes these people are not even aware that traffic has started moving again! They are still sitting there, resigned to just surviving.

THE SOURCE OF SATISFACTION

Satisfaction comes from within, not from external sources, such as the acknowledgement you get from others. Whatever agreement or acknowledgment you get from others is not satisfying, in and of itself. Agreement is merely peer approval of being "okay" or of being acceptable by other people's standards—it is not satisfaction. Genuine satisfaction is a very personal experience—a very personal victory. Of course, there is a bonus if you can share it with others, but you are the source of it. Your attitude is the victory.

I like the analogy of picturing life as a bus, where you can be either the bus driver or one of the passengers. Being the driver and knowing exactly where you are going (the route you will be taking with its stops and detours) gives you a sense of control and certainty about reaching your destination.

As a passenger who isn't certain of the schedule and route, you would be likely to miss out on any satisfying accomplishment. You wouldn't seem to be able to do anything about the results and you couldn't be certain about how the destination would be reached anyway.

In the bus of life, you have a total choice whether to be the bus driver or a passenger. Of course, the driver also gets to make wrong turns, driving errors, and mistakes; he also gets the prize, the "win" of pulling off a successful trip, getting *where he wanted to go, when he wanted to get there.*

In this book, I have attempted to provide you with all the necessary know-how to become the bus driver in the bus of life. The goal of this book is to support you in recognizing what you want, but it cannot make you do it. That is up to you alone.

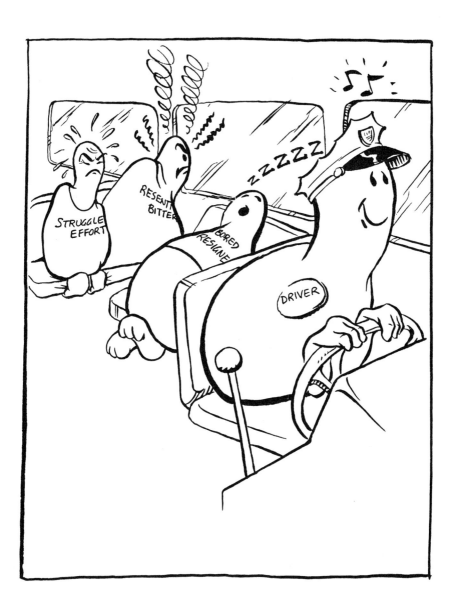

THE BUS OF LIFE

I like a state of continued becoming, with a goal in front and not behind.

George Bernard Shaw

CHAPTER II

DISCOVERING WHAT WE WANT

Discovering what things we want is a truly exhilarating experience—a joy, a delight, a true discovery process! Many people possess an attitude that spelling out what they want would be burdensome, adding work or assignments or new loads to an already hectic life-schedule.

I have found that the opposite is true, however—that barriers are released and it becomes a lightening process: TAKING AWAY burdens that prevent us from fully experiencing our lives.

We can look to teachers and prophets, psychologists and gurus, or others outside of ourselves for the answers. However, the answers are all inside us and discovering them can be a ball! Only *we* can define *our* own happiness. As William Shakespeare wrote, "How bitter a thing it is to look into happiness through another man's eyes!"

Looking outside of ourselves for what we want is an automatic point of view that keeps us separate from what we want. It gets in the way.

Looking into our innerself maintains the "oneness" that keeps us in charge of our own universe—*where we are and what we want.*

And, we don't have to depend on others for our happiness—we don't have to ask Santa Claus for it!

It is important that our goals are our very own and nobody else's. Our intentions need to be expressed out of who *we* are, not what we think we *should* be. If we are concerned about "shoulds," we create a detached point of view—a separateness that prevents or blocks us from what we want—a frustrating experience at best!

If you asked a thousand people from a typical sampling of our society, "What do you want in your life?", the vast majority would pause and then utter somewhat confusedly, "You know, I really don't know!" Try it on some friends and you will witness this phenomenon yourself.

11

Amazing, isn't it? With all of our modern education and advanced technology on *how* to accomplish what we want, or *how* to get the results we want, we have made so little progress in the area of recognizing *what* it is that we want!

Of those who may reply to our question with real, positive answers, most would probably say, "All I want is to be happy." A few others would likely include "being loved" and "being happy." Maybe, just maybe, *one person* out of our sampling of one thousand would be able to clearly state what he or she wanted, listing *specific personal goals.*

As a consultant, I frequently worked with clients on a one-to-one basis, utilizing the Focusing technique. During these private, individual Focusing appointments, most clients would start off with three or four goals they seemed to be very clear about. Ironically, this clarity was usually the result of preparing themselves for the Focusing session. By the time they'd completed our appointment and looked at all the areas of their lives, this list had usually grown ten to twenty times in size!

On an average, my Focusing clients would leave with eighty or ninety very specific goals. Quite often their lists exceeded one hundred items that they considered important enough to be listed! It seemed that once the looking process started, once people recognized that all those wants and desires were there (and they acknowledged them), a vast and unlimited flow of desires would open up. This would appear to be proof positive that most of us hold back on true desires, keeping them out of our everyday thoughts. We keep them covered up and hidden in the lower reaches of our subconscious.

People have a tendency to deny their true desires, to invalidate their wants, and to explain or rationalize away any "unusual" dreams or fantasies.

From what I've observed, the most common barrier that people have placed between their desires and their existing personal realities are (1) their unwillingness to confront the possibility of failing and (2) the belief that they don't deserve to get what they want.

There are many other barriers, I am sure, but these two seem to be the chief blocks for people in acknowledging their own desires.

Worrying about what others may think is another popular barrier that encompasses a fear of ridicule or being ostracized by one's peers. Feeling "too silly" or presumptuous and other similar social acceptance fears interfere with people's ability to see what they really want for themselves.

DENYING WHAT YOU WANT, FOR WHATEVER JUSTIFICATION, CAN PRODUCE UNDERLYING DISCONTENT AND AN ATTITUDE THAT WILL ROB YOU OF A SATISFYING LIFE!

Actress Marlo Thomas, during a TV interview several years ago, spoke about her experiences regarding what people say about going after things that may have seemed impossible or somehow unattainable. She said, "People want you to 'face the facts.' I know the ledger is full of lots of reasons why I shouldn't do this *and* I'd like to give it a go anyway." This kind of personal integrity and dedication to having things the way you want them is what it takes to make your life start working more *perfectly.*

I often hear people complain that they look and look but can't really see what they want. I envision this scene where people are standing on a beach, gazing out to the horizon, waiting for THE GOAL to appear, as though there is one very significant goal they *should* have and it will come rising out of the distance like some sort of Hollywood movie monster. My Focusing clients generally discovered an enormous inventory of desires which they spilled out from within themselves, apparent proof that our goals are there waiting within us. They just need to be jarred loose.

The "self" portion of us, the *supreme being* in all of us, the *natural knowing* that is a part of our very essence, our *complete being* possesses the absolute ability to know what we want—to recognize our intentions in life. **ALL WE NEED TO DO IN ORDER TO RECOGNIZE WHAT WE WANT IS TO REMOVE ALL THE CLUTTER COVERING UP OUR TRUE INTENTIONS!**

THE "I SHOULD" SYNDROME

From my own experience in creating goal-setting programs, I've observed that one of the chief robbers of satisfaction in people's lives seems to be a general sense of conflict that results from what people think they *should* want and what they really *do* want.

Seldom, if ever, do people have any sense of their own personal wants and desires. Usually, they end up with a definite *decision* as to what they *should* want, and this is generally associated with a real resistance to looking at what they *really* do want.

As more people verbalized on the subject, it became clearer and clearer to me that they didn't want what they thought they *should* have wanted. What they really wanted eventually came to the surface. The conflict between what they *really* wanted and what they felt they *should* have wanted invariably resulted in their feeling wrong for not wanting what they thought they should. Can you see how much less satisfying this was for them? Seeking out a goal you think you *should* want rather than going for something that really *is you* can be very unexciting.

A very typical example of this kind of unrewarding "should-ness" can be seen in millions of marriages. A sizeable majority of married people with whom I have consulted realized that they initially got married, chose their spouse and lived their early married years conforming to a *picture,* or a concept, of how they were "supposed to" live life. In the case of my women clients, they chose the bright handsome young man with a future; the men married "fairy princesses" just like in all the nursery rhymes. Isn't that the way everybody did it when they went off "to live happily ever after"?

Many of the single people I have consulted with have not made that mistake—they are making a different kind of mistake. They're still looking for the mate to fit the picture of who they "should" marry, probably at the expense of some very rewarding relationships with others who don't fit their pictures.

The "I should" behavior is a product of what our minds conjure up, based on social agreement for our own ideas of what (we think) other people might think. One of the most outstanding and popular examples of this syndrome (that many people have shared with me) is that people felt they should be continuously striving to make great amounts of money when, in reality, they had no great desire to have a lot of money! Many people, particularly men, go through a majority of their lifetime considering themselves failures for not conforming to this picture of the self-made business tycoon.

Did you ever notice that the man who seemingly has everything—a million dollars, a Rolls Royce, etc.—still finds life somewhat unsatisfying? How many times have you heard the expression, "Yes, but is he really happy?" This paints a picture of happiness or, as I prefer, satisfaction as being totally illusory, evading both the rich and the poor, the middle income people, and everybody else. Sounds reasonable, right? If happiness evades even the rich and powerful, then is must be *absolutely* illusory and unavailable to all of mankind. There now. Now we have a *very reasonable explanation* for not being rich or happy. Wow, this is some myth we have created!

14

HAVE FUN

Discovering your goals, uncovering them from under all that previous conditioning and denial can be a wonderful experience! Never look at goals as a burden, look at them as an adventure! The attitude that setting goals is a heavy, tedious experience does exist in our society. In fact, it is even quite popular. So you can set yourself apart from the masses by looking at goal-setting as a light, invigorating adventure and by having a good time at it.

Maria, a delightful woman who first came to me as a Focusing client and, subsequently, became a very good friend, shared with me that she had worked for a very popular, world-famous success and sales training organization, and that she had spent three weeks looking at her own goals in their sales training courses. After completing the course, she was more convinced than ever that goals needed to be heavy and significant burdens to be tolerated in order to be a success—something you HAD TO DO in order to succeed.

Maria had previously compared goal-setting to taking medicine—something you did that was a real drag, but it made you *better.* You didn't enjoy it but it was something you were *supposed* to do. Her experience upon completing Focusing was that she left me smiling radiantly and raving about how exciting it was to have experienced discovering her goals.

A similar popular concept of goals was paraphrased by Neal, a professional writer, who suggested the analogy of Superman putting off cleaning the Kryptonite out of his closet. For those of you who followed the adventures of Superman, you'll recall that Kryptonite was a mineral from a far-off planet that robbed the fictional superhero of his superhuman strength. Could Superman be guilty of procrastination? Why not? Could we be superpeople if we cleaned out closets?

Getting closer on what we want is like Superman confronting his Kryptonite. It may be resisted at first, but it represents an act that needs to happen if our full potential is ever going to be realized.

On a more personal level, you do have an *absolute choice* in how to look at what you want in life—your goals.

● You can look at them as medicine (to be taken in order to get better, as Maria did), or . . .

● You can look at them as an adventure, a joy of discovery!

You can choose which way you'd like to think of them. It's just a matter of your attitude. Think of how a sailboat manages to travel in either direction, regardless of which way the winds are blowing. The *attitude* of the sails determines the direction. You can take control, or drift—it's up to you.

WHAT IS A GOAL?

Simply stated, a goal is a target, a point of completion for a predetermined desire or want, a place where we can see if our intentions are being realized. Our minds want to see the light at the end of the tunnel. It is extremely difficult for us to get motivated about making any progress towards an unknown target. Without the target, we tend to stop progressing and just exist. We tend to drift aimlessly, just taking what comes our way.

Art, a highly respected man in the California media and statewide political scene, provided me with a great definition of a goal, during our Focusing session. He said, "A goal is a statement of intention." What a great definition! Our goals are truly a measure of our desire to see something happen in our lives—to see the results we want.

A goal does not need to be a physical object or wealth. A goal is anything we want— any *thing,* any *action,* any *condition,* any *experience,* quality in our lives. A goal is where you deliver your potential—you know, that *stuff* you keep walking around with. That stuff that people keep writing about. Potential sitting in storage, unused, is about the most senseless waste of energy I can imagine, millions of times more needless than leaving the lights on all night, driving gas-guzzling cars, or wasting other forms of chemical or mineral energy. In my opinion, human potential is the biggest waste of energy on this planet, including oil, electricity, and natural gas!

Not only is human potential being wasted; it happens to be a lot of effort to keep it in the potential form—rather than releasing it—converting it to kinetic or active energy.

"THERE IS NO HEAVIER BURDEN THAN A GREAT POTENTIAL."

This famous line was uttered by one of the modern world's great philosophers. It appeared in thousands of newspapers around the world and was syndicated internationally. It was spoken by the Peanuts comic strip character, Linus, as one of his grand philosophies during a baseball game. Even though it was spoken by Charles Schulz's cartoon character, this statement is really worth thinking about. Having the potential to manifest something that we want in our lives—and not having it—is truly very burdensome. It truly does require more energy to keep under wraps than to release.

It is work—a lot of work—to walk around with energy that is not being utilized. So why not release it and let it out? Who needs the burden? Who needs the storage space filled with wasted energy?

Goals are wants, desires, dreams, things we'd like to see in ourselves, in our lives, and in our environment.

Goals are truly personal. They are declarations of our own personal intentions in life. Goals can also be professional, if that is what we personally desire. Goals can be set for our own internal sense of ourselves. Goals can be set for how we relate to others. Goals can be set for how we want others to relate to us. Goals can be expressed for the kind of person we want to be. Goals can be expressed for the things we want to have. Goals can be expressed for what we want to do.

Goals are a vital part of who we are. Goals are our own personal aims and targets that we want for ourselves, even though it sometimes looks like we want them for others.

Goals are the fuel of a satisfying life. To have no goals is like running out of gas and being parked on the planet like an abandoned car, waiting to be towed away. Why not make life as interesting, as challenging, as satisfying as you can? Why not express all your goals? Why not get them all out there so you have a full tank of gas, so that you are fully energized?

GOALS: THE DESTINATIONS

In your present form, in the body you presently occupy, this lifetime is the only shot you get. So, why not go for it? I was profoundly impressed by a sign in the Museum at the Jack London State Historic Park in Glen Ellen, California. The placard quoted the world-famous author who had demonstrated a real lust for living in his short, forty-year life.

Two months before he died, in September 1916, London stated, "The proper function of a man is to *live,* not *exist.* I shall use my time."

This is the only chance you will ever have on this exciting adventure called life. Why not plan it, try to live it as richly, as happily as possible?

Dale Carnegie

CHAPTER III

HOW WE'VE DONE SO FAR

Once our basic needs are assured, there exists a human tendency to become discontented, taking our basic needs for granted. As Maslow states in *Motivation and Personality,* "We have learned that one of the possible consequences of basic need gratification may be boredom, aimlessness, anomie, and the like. Apparently we function best when we are striving for something we lack, when we wish for something that we do not have, and when we organize our powers of striving for the gratification of that wish."

He continues to describe how the state of being gratified does not necessarily guarantee utopia or contentment, but how often it provides only temporary happiness, which then tends to be followed by another and possibly higher state of discontent.

Maslow observes that happiness seems illusory and suggests that we accept its "intrinsic transience," especially if we look at its higher forms such as "peak experiences" and other states of intense happiness which are episodic.

This would seem totally contradictory to the theory of happiness that we have promoted all of our lives—where the handsome prince and the fairy princess live happily ever after—the illusion that there is a condition in life called "external happiness," which, when reached, will not require any more from us.

Maslow calls this his Grumble Theory, whereby most people find the only meaningful life to be striving for something they do not have. He excluded those very rare self-actualized people who can "live in the realm of Being." Maslow observed, "It looks as if the human hope for external happiness can never be fulfilled."

Dissatisfaction is a necessary ingredient if satisfaction is the condition being sought. There can be no satisfaction unless there is dissatisfaction. It is similar in concept to the impossibility of there being no "down" if there is no "up"; no "truth" without "lies";

no "empty" if there is no "full"; no "success" without "failure"; etc.

Satisfaction is gained from progressing towards a desired end, from a point of view which (by definition) needs to represent *dissatisfaction.* Why would we be progressing towards "A," if being at "non-A" was totally satisfying? Apparently, we need to be somehow discontented with "non-A" if we want to reach "A."

The game of satisfaction is to maximize the "high" enjoyable satisfying moments and minimize those unsatisfying times. I can be having a ball, feeling very high and invigorated, while working in a condition or an environment that I find undesirable. I sense I am making progress toward my goal, or the ultimate condition that I want to exist. If I am content where I am, why would I be moving towards something else? Therefore, discontent or undesirability needs to exist in order to have a desired result that is more significant or more desirable. If I am not sensing progress, or if all these little "moments of satisfaction" disappear, then I can get bogged down in a static state of dissatisfaction, which can be a real drag. I'm not saying that the existing state, the one I am moving *from,* is intolerable or that I feel my survival is somehow threatened by it. I'm saying that the existing state is just *less desirable* —I am chosing a more preferable or a more desirable state—a goal.

IS YOUR CLOCK TICKING?

Think about a nonelectric, hand-wound clock. While you may not notice the progress the hands are making and you may be unable to perceive any motion, you know that progress is being made as long as you hear it ticking. When it stops ticking, you know that progress has ceased.

Goals can be like winding your clock. The potential energy that is stored inside of you when you have a goal can start you ticking and demonstrate to you that the clock is running again.

Visualize yourself as an alarm clock—one you have designed yourself. You have prepared it and maintained it well and it is in perfect working order; you really enjoy the sound of the alarm as it goes off. You even like where the clock is located in the room and how it complements its surroundings. Now, you'd like to hear the alarm more frequently!

Your aims, goals, intentions, wants, and desires for the future are what wind your clock. You can set the alarm as frequently as you would like now, because the clock is totally energized by your desire to see something happen. Some people may want to hear the alarm (realize a goal) every other day. Some may need to hear the alarm every hour; some may require more time and feel the result worth waiting for, setting their alarm for years in advance. But the clock needs to be wound all the time or the alarm will never ring!

Higher and more challenging goals are frequently necessary to raise the ante of the game, in order to keep ourselves interested. While current goals are being reached, new goals need to be set in order to keep our juices flowing, to keep us feeling alive, satisfied, invigorated, and interested,

Dr. Arnold A. Hutschnecker, author of *The Drive for Power, The Will to Live,* and *The Will to Happiness,* is a noted psychiatrist who has studied the potential for human improvement with great dedication. In addressing the topic of the American Dream, Dr. Hutschnecker writes, "A man, if he does not want to fade away, must go on creating values that equal his degree of maturity. Goals and objectives change, as does a man's pace. But there is a need to shift gears or there will be inner turmoil, emptiness, or death in the rocking chair."

STAGNATION

If the clock runs down, or new goals are not expressed, or the new goals are not challenging enough for us, a number of conditions may manifest themselves.

One very common condition is the one we label "boredom," a feeling of absolute "putting up with it all," certainly lacking in aliveness and originality. Many people work very hard at *not being bored,* which is a form of a goal, I suppose, but it seems to be originating from a questionable source—the desire for a lack of a negative-oriented state rather than the positive desired state.

Being bored is only a negative condition if you chose it to be. Some people I know view boredom as the worst condition possible and therefore are motivated by "not being bored." So they spend their time keeping busy and maintaining very hectic schedules—to avoid boredom—rather than engaging in activities because they want to. This is much like *winning* solely in order to avoid *losing*. Setting goals in order to avoid boredom is a form of fear motivation—the fear of being bored.

Another very common condition is apathy, or an "I really don't care" kind of resignation. This is very much like boredom, but with less negative evaluation attached to it, so that the person just "hangs out" with how things are, not caring. I have observed two distinctly different types regarding apathetic people, the result of not having any significance or importance assigned to anything at all in life.

APATHETIC TYPE I

Charles was a perfect example of one type of an apathetic person. He played the role of being supermellow and easy-going, fun-loving, and casual; he never admitted that anything was of any importance to him. Whatever way things turned out—it was okay with him. He didn't care, or admit to caring, about *anything* at all.

He was active and "busy," doing a lot of things that people do when they are having fun. He expressed a willingness to take whatever came. On those rare occasions when he expressed his desires, he inevitably stated them as "I would kind-of-like to . . . ." He seldom stated firmly and positively what he wanted to do. But he was "cool." He would never seem disappointed because he put out no expectations for things to happen. He was avoiding disappointment by not ever expecting anything, never expressing a desire for something.

APATHETIC TYPE II

The more conspicuous type of person who demonstrates the other type of apathetic behavior doesn't go anywhere, doesn't see much of anyone, and doesn't seem to be having much fun. These people are not only implying, "I'm bored and I don't care," but also, "If you don't mind, I'll quit." This attitude doesn't seem to have any economic boundaries. I've seen this behavior in swank, elegant mansions and in city slums. It seems to have no socioeconomic commonality.

The most obvious example of this form of apathy (in the poverty extreme) is the wino, panhandler, or street bum. These people seem to have dropped out of life as they saw it, and have quit participating in the mainstream of society. While watching a very touching interview of a down-and-out panhandler on a TV news special one evening, it occurred to me that the man being interviewed just didn't give a damn about anything! He not only didn't care, but he didn't care that he didn't care.

On the other side of this socioeconomic scale we have all the wealthy people who have become apathetic. To self-made people, this condition or attitude is often too unacceptable for their own standards, so they end up as suicides, alcoholics, or some other "upper class" form of a dropout. Quite often, people who are considered highly successful by society's standards find themselves in this behavior pattern, frequently by accident, when they are not currently engaged in satisfying pursuits, yet feel they must keep up their image or the appearance that they are still just as successful as they once were. They are usually people who thought that everything would be okay when they reached a certain plateau and then discovered it really wasn't. They don't get that what they are looking for is in the getting there, not the place they get to.

IT'S CONTAGIOUS

As a static state, dissatisfaction also demonstrates itself through unsupportive attitudes towards others. I've seen people who have lost their sense of purpose or direction for themselves altogether, who then begin sabotaging their friends, fellow workers, neighbors, and relatives. This undermining of people they care for is most usually unconscious (it is not a preconceived or planned behavior to destroy the satisfaction available to others), but nevertheless occurs.

Resentment of other people's success seems to be a common trait for people who have slowed up or stopped seeking improvement in the quality of their own lives. It can be demonstrated through a variety of sly skills we have learned over the years. Jealousy of others who seem to be having more fun or who seem to be experiencing life in a more rewarding way is not an uncommon reaction.

At some time in almost everybody's life, an attitude will crop up where the level of their experience, the quality of their life, is mistakenly attributed to some source outside themselves. I've been at this point many times myself and I have observed this to be a very common tendency. It includes a feeling like everybody and everything is controlling your life. Many people stay in this frame of mind all their lives! It has been called "being at effect"—the opposite of "being cause" in how your life works.

People who are "at effect" want to blame others for what is happening to them. They want to explain and provide lists of reasons for their situation by dramatizing how someone else is responsible for it.

Totally energized goal-oriented people tend to do this far less frequently since they are more in control of everything that affects their lives, by virtue of being the designers of how their lives work.

Another sign of dissatisfaction that I have personally experienced has been what could be called "the blahs." This is a feeling I can best describe by a lack of energy, laziness, and a diminished desire to socialize.

The blahs are different from apathy, as I see them, in that they are usually temporary feelings of low energy. This empty unfulfilled feeling is another characteristic that many people have observed in themselves when they have no conscious desire to be working towards anything. This feeling was once described to me by a client as the "is that all there is?" feeling. She recalled the popular song of the 1960s by the same name, recorded by songstress Peggy Lee, and compared her attitude with the attitude Miss Lee vocalized in the song.

For my own personal life, this syndrome best describes the attitude I held for nearly two years, in the early 1970s. I had always been a very energetic person and I considered myself to be quite the entrepreneurial wheeler-dealer. In my mid-twenties, I set out to do many things I considered exciting, that looked challenging, and represented a lot of fun, particularly things that could be organized as businesses. I figured that if I did all these things, with all the energy I had, that I'd make a ton of money and could retire by the age of 35. Well, I was real dynamo! I started numerous businesses, all very glamorous, that looked like they had a high potential for profit. In fact, I managed to start over 30 ventures between 1964 and 1972, including corporations, partnerships, and my own sole proprietorships. These ventures included real estate development, promotion and advertising, newspaper publishing, personal management, a production company, and several ventures in motor sports. I was a regular achievement-machine and I fascinated myself with how many things I could have going on at the same time. At one time, I was a major stockholder and a member of the Board of Directors of three corporations, an owner of two of my own separate businesses, and had five ventures waiting on the back burner.

In late 1972, a series of personal incidents highlighted a period of my life when I suddenly became aware that I was running out of satisfying things to do. While I had some fantastic memories and a list of tremendous ego-oriented accomplishments that were the rival of many of my peers, I found myself unmotivated to continue on this path. Recalling the good times was not enough. I wanted the excitement, the challenges, and the outrageousness back again. It seemed as though I had lost my creativity and originality of ideas.

I spent two to three years in this state—a state of "is that all there is?" At the time, it seemed to me that I had done it all—all those things I thought I wanted to do as a youth of 16. I developed a romantic relationship to which I devoted most of my energy, while maintaining an office with its related expense overhead that just *looked* at new projects but never really *did* anything! Business itself became a pure overhead function for me. I was just going through the motions. As this condition persisted, I began to judge myself and make myself "wrong" for losing my spark and incentive. Now, I see that I simply quit setting new goals! I had done this so automatically before that I didn't realize it at the time.

Another dissatisfying attitude that can be contagious is frequently demonstrated by people who dream about things they want, but never look at having them in their lives.

I prefer to picture a *dream* as a higher form of goal—a goal of particular significance for the dreamer. For a storekeeper who works long, hard hours, it could be early retirement. For a mother who has raised a family under tenement conditions, it could be a brand new home. For a teenage beauty queen, it might be a date with a movie idol. If a person wants to call these kinds of goals his or her dreams, then, so be it. However, if a person continually holds out dreams as things to be desired, wished for or hoped for *without* any reality of their coming true, *without* ever seeing them as becoming real, then discontent will most certainly grow. The context in which these dreams are held, by the very attitude of the dreamer, will prevent them from becoming real. By holding them in the context of *not being possible,* you will cut yourself off from the possibility of their ever becoming real for you.

Dissatisfaction and discontent are only of value in order to motivate us to doing something about it—to progress toward what we want, away from what we don't want. If we hold out dreams with no intention of having them become real for us, we are guaranteeing ourselves a life of diminished satisfaction. Not only will we not be getting what we want out of life, we will spend most of the time in our dreams and fantasies rather than totally experiencing what is going on in our present reality.

Another example of the "dream wished for" attitude, and also an external answer or explanation for not being as happy as we could be, is the attitude that "All I need is _____ and everything will be great." I know many people who fill this blank space with some condition that they never intend to have in their lives. Then they have a good reason for their life to be the way it is. It becomes "explainable."

"Boy, if I weren't married, would I have a ball!" How many times have you heard that? These kinds of everyday, light-hearted statements indicate how eager people are to accept mediocrity or dissatisfying conditions in their lives. In the above quip, the person making the statement has generally made absolutely sure he or she will be staying married, and, therefore, *not having a ball.* Usually, there is no real intention to get divorced. If that ever did happen, the person would then be *required* to "have a ball" in order to keep his or her word and save face with friends and other confidantes. Think of how awesome it could be to demonstrate to all your friends, beyond a doubt, that you were "having a ball," should you leave your spouse. That could be embarrassing if you ever needed to deliver—to *really* show your friends.

WHAT THE "EXPERTS" SAY

By getting clearer about what you want and completing the Focusing process, you will be doing what many professional organizations do for themselves with regard to company objectives and goals. In essence, you are approaching your life professionally—like a professional "liver." There are some "experts" in the business, who generally make their livings selling their knowledge to business organizations, rather than individuals. Let's hear what some of them have to say about goals.

Paul J. Meyer, the man who founded Success Motivation Institute (SMI), has stated that "goal-setting is the strongest human force for self-motivation." He states further that "it is obvious that goal-setting is essential to success."

Alan Lakein, renowned time-management expert and author of *How to Get Control of Your Time and Your Life,* makes a very concrete statement about a personal goals list. "It will give a direction to your life. It will help you feel in control of your destiny."

E. James Rohn, founder of another achievement and motivational organization, Adventures in Achievement, leads seminars all over the world. He has stated, "One of the most important things I ever learned was how to set goals."

Dr. Maxwell Maltz writes in *Psycho-Cybernetics* that "we find no real satisfaction or happiness in life without obstacles to conquer and goals to achieve. People who say that life is not worthwhile are really saying that they themselves have no personal goals which are worthwhile . . ."

Werner Erhard is a man for whom I hold a tremendous amount of admiration and respect. He founded the *est* organization in 1971 and it has become a modern age phenomenon in the human potential movement since then. I had the privilege to be associated with this organization in 1974 and 1975. One of Werner's observations that I find particularly appropriate here is "To master life, you simply need to know what you want." How simple can you make it?

". . . life planning is useless, unless at the end of the process we are very definite about exactly what we want to do—for now and beyond." This statement was written by Richard Nelson Bolles and included in his book *What Color Is Your Parachute?*, which many people have found valuable reading while considering new careers.

Dr. Jack H. Grossman is the author of *The Business of Living,* a book about running your life as if it were your own business. I am particularly fond of one line by Dr. Grossman which states, "Living is the business of making desires and dreams come true."

All of these words by experts and masters at maximizing the potential we all possess are included here in order to dramatize just how essential it is to be clear and certain about what you want, in order to experience satisfaction and fulfillment while attaining it.

ABOUT WINNING

Did you ever notice the degree of satisfaction that you feel when you win at something? Do you feel really exceptional sometimes, yet a little empty at other times? A Focusing client once pointed out to me how she hardly ever felt very good about winning at tennis. Mary was quite good, was much better than her opponents. "It seems so hollow, sometimes," she told me during a goals session. "I beat them easily and I get very little out of it," she complained, wondering why her victories were not more satisfying.

At first, this seemed somewhat curious, since the great American victory habit is supposed to produce super amounts of satisfaction. As we talked further, however, Mary saw more and more clearly of herself that she was beating her opponents out of a *fear of losing* rather than performing in alignment with her own self-determined goals. Given her motivation, therefore, she tended to hang back and play with people who were less threatening to her, people she knew she could beat. Wanting "not to lose" is another robber of satisfaction. Rather than playing the game, enjoying the game, and going for her own goals, Mary was playing to beat someone else in order "not to be a loser." Instead of satisfaction, she ended up with "not being a loser."

This is a very *fine* point, but very *significant* when it comes to the rewards of living a satisfying life. If you didn't get the point, I want you to go back and reread the last paragraph. The picture of the event may be the same, but the experience of the winner can be totally different.

FEAR MOTIVATION

While I acknowledge the existence of fear motivation to promote winning, especially in sports, I do not support it. I prefer self-motivation, using our own personal goals and desires for our own performance to be the motivation behind our accomplishments.

Heisman trophy winner and retired football star O. J. Simpson has stated that "fear of losing is what helps make competitors great." O. J. continued, "Show me a gracious loser and I'll show you a perennial loser. I'll show class, but I take losing hard."

O. J. 's philosophy, as demonstrated in this statement and his extraordinary performance, is proof that fear motivation produces "winners," but I suggest that winning can be far more satisfying and much more fun if the motivation comes from a source closer to one's own identity and sense of self, rather than fear of nonacceptance, of rejection, or of being labeled a "loser."

Personal goals can provide an even more powerful incentive than fear and, in the future, I expect to see more and more athletes and coaches working on this positive approach to motivating physical performance. A very good friend of mine, author Phillip Finch, provided me with some insights about how Decathlon champion Bruce Jenner motivates himself. Phil was writing the book on Bruce's rise to becoming "The World's Greatest Athlete," during the 1976 Olympics where the young Californian won the gold medal. According to Phil, Bruce had his own individual goals for each of his performances for each of the ten Decathlon events in which he competed. He set out to accomplish personal records for himself and was able to enjoy the real fruits of winning—out of *his own desire,* not out of fear!

WHAT PEOPLE GO THROUGH

There are thousands of very good "reasons" that people use to explain the compromises, scarcity, and mediocrity in their lives when it comes to things (or desires) they want for themselves. They can give you all the explanations for why they don't have what they want. They can list all the excuses for what is preventing them from having things the way they want them. They are usually very "reasonable" and much "agreement" can be seen around them.

FAILURE-DISAPPOINTMENT

One of the most popular explanations for why people don't get clear about what they want for themselves is that they wouldn't want to experience the disappointment that would occur should they fail to get it.

Think of how many people you know who graduated from college, after a number of years of specialized training in something they enjoyed, and yet never found their way into the professional community to earn a living in the field in which they were trained.

How many people do you know who are still in jobs that they took as a matter of convenience years ago! Charles took a part-time job while working in high school. He stayed with the same job while going to college. He is still working at the same trade today, over twenty years later, even though he received a professional degree in another subject entirely. I am not criticizing Charles' behavior, so long as he was making a free choice in the matter and really enjoyed and received value from what he was doing.

In the case of Charles, however, it seemed to be a matter of staying comfortable in a familiar position rather than running a risk of discomfort or failure in venturing into something new. On many occasions, he shared with me how much he disliked his position and how he wanted to do something else, nothing specific. Still, he went on and on, staying where he'd been. Does this sound familiar? Do you know anyone like this?

WHAT WILL HAPPEN WITH MY FRIENDS?

People will also hold themselves back in order to maintain acceptance of their peers. Many of my Focusing clients shared with me that they were afraid of losing their friends if they started having a more prosperous life, having more fun, enjoying life more, etc. Afraid that their friends will think them pompous, or superior in some way, many people maintain a reasonable explanation for staying exactly where they are. As a result, they associate with people with whom they feel "comfortable" in this kind of behavior, a basic level of *lessened achievement*. Therefore, the group as a whole tends to maintain a level of mediocrity, or a level where things are less desirable.

Dave discovered a great desire to be a financial success, but was afraid that his friends would ostracize him for being successful. He felt terribly attached to this group of friends who seldom had money and, therefore, seemed unwilling to do anything that might not meet with their approval. As a result, he felt a total conflict between something he actually desired (financial success) and another thing that he seemed to need, his continued relationship with his friends.

SANTA CLAUS

A common idea people have about listing goals is that "it's like asking Santa Claus for what I want for Christmas." Well, it's not a lot unlike that! When we were asked for Christmas lists for Santa in our childhood, we wanted some source *outside of ourselves* to provide us with items we considered significant and important to our well-being at the time. Writing out a list of what we want still signifies things we consider worthwhile and valuable to our well-being at this time, but there is a difference in where we place the responsibility for the source of it.

GOOD TIMES/BAD TIMES

The following exercise can be extremely enjoyable and has been found to be so by many of my clients in the past:

Make a list of all the things at which you are really skilled. Keep looking for all kinds of activities about which you are not only confident, but *superior.*

In addition to listing all of the excellent skills you possess, list all the things that you truly enjoy doing or that you really "get off on." Spend at least five minutes on this. Next, make a list of all the things you *do not* enjoy doing and that you *are not* well-skilled at. Spend at least five minutes on this list as well.

Now, compare the lists. In looking at these two lists, notice which items your peer group or friends would agree you *should* or *should not* like. Notice which items on the list your friends would approve, acknowledge you for, in terms of abilities. Do you enjoy other things besides the ones your friends acknowledge you for? Can you begin to get a sense of how you may have held yourself back from being who you really are because you might offend or somehow become separated from your friends or your family?

GOOD HARD WORKER

An incredibly large number of people are dedicated to just getting by, while being "good hard working" people. They all share a belief that if you work hard and stick to it, life will work out. Well, that's great for people who want to be *good hard workers,* but make certain that's really what you want to be. If you want to get what you want, however, and maximize your effectiveness, then check to see if you've fallen into the "good hard worker" trap.

It has been my own experience that most people want to produce the greatest results in the least amount of time. To accomplish this kind of effectiveness, the image of a toiling, midnight-oil burning, superbusy, working machine has to be severely modified— preferably done away with completely. Time management experts agree that we waste enormous portions of our daily lives fulfilling good hard worker pictures, keeping busy and accomplishing tasks that have nothing to do with our primary objectives.

So, how about it? Do you want to be known as a "good hard worker" or as a person who gets what you want?

Hoyt Axton, a popular country-Western singer, sings a song that goes

". . . work your fingers to the bone, what do you get? Bony fingers!"

There is some irony in the chorus of this song also. The words seem to be indicative, a perfect example of another of the syndromes of the "good hard workers"—hoping it will all work out. The chorus goes:

"Maybe things will get a little better in the morning."

People who subscribe to the "good hard worker" philosophy consistency manifest themselves in business as hard-charging, committed and aggressive dynamos. In relationships, these people manifest this belief by always having problems or misunderstandings with their spouse, lover, or friend. They feel that they need to work at relationships and, of course, they are "good hard workers." Otherwise, there would be no struggle or work involved.

Regarding having nice things in their environment, some subscribers to the "good hard worker" philosophy create realities that include suffering, illness, or other problems so that their friends won't think of them as being *too lucky* or *too well-off.* After all, if you don't have problems, it can't be too worthwhile, right?

"Life is a struggle, life is hard," these people will say, *and* they truly believe it! I guarantee you that for as long as they believe that life is hard, they will do everything they can do to prove that their beliefs are justified. They will do this subconsciously, of course, but they will make sure that their lives provides accurate testimony to what they *believe*—that life *is* hard. They will cause struggle to justify their prosperity. They will work harder to justify their successes. They will not allow themselves to simply be totally satisfied *without a struggle and hard work!*

WHAT FUN SHOULD BE

COMFORT

Our society, as a whole, seems to have one outstanding common goal. However, I have observed no satisfaction in it whatsoever. In fact, I don't know anyone who has found any satisfaction in it and yet everyone seems to be going after it like a herd of buffalo. The goal I am addressing is the goal of being *comfortable.* More people suffer grave disappointment upon reaching "the comfortable life," especially after subscribing to the hard work and struggle philosophy, than from any other area of misplaced or misjudged expectations.

As human beings, we even tend to *stay* comfortable, once we've attained the state, even when we realize it isn't all that hot, anyway! We have learned to seek out comfort to such an extent that we often have comfort connected to the ultimate purpose in life—that is, our ultimate purpose often appears to be "becoming comfortable."

I'm reminded of an experiment in which scientists had microscopically observed amoebas in two distinctly different environments. One environment was totally stimulus-free, the laboratory equivalent of absolute and total comfort for the amoeba. The other environment was one of constant stimulus where the amoeba was continually in a state of agitation. This environment represented discomfort.

Now, picture the comparison—a living cellular structure in a state of total *comfort* with all environmental conditions, such as temperature, humidity, and light, at the ideal point, and another living organism in a perpetual state of upset, or an environment of *discomfort,* having all these conditions at extremely agitating levels.

Ironically, both amoebas died in their environments. Doesn't this suggest that it takes *some comfort* and *some discomfort,* in a mix, for life to continue? If so, it seems the problems, upsets, and other occurrences that are discomforting at times may actually be necessary to our basic survival! We might actually require upsets, problems, and other discomforting conditions. Yet, as a society, we seek the absence of these conditions as optimum!

Most people see comfort as the ultimate goal, and they wonder why it seems so unrewarding when they become more and more comfortable. Of course, comfort means different things to many different people. Security, vacations, furnishings and clothes, and things that do everything for us automatically, are all popular ideas of being comfortable. But, seeking total comfort can be as deadly and destructive as seeking total discomfort, or death.

As soon as a situation in your life becomes comfortable, boredom and apathy come into play. Your mind has difficulty conceiving that it's time to get uncomfortable, and move to a new plateau. This sounds totally unreasonable and most of the time beyond our mind's ability to understand it. It makes "better sense," to our minds, to stay in a comfortable position. At least, this is what our previous conditioning has suggested all our lives. When things get too uncomfortable, we tend to stop, quit, stay comfortable. We tend to do this in all of our activities.

As a result, people *relate* to one another up to a point where they start to feel uncomfortable. Then they tend to stop—to go no further. These persons are now limited by their compulsion to stay comfortable as to who they associate with, who their neighbors are, the kinds of jobs and fellow employees they work with, the family they create for themselves, the personal relationships in which they engage, etc.

Staying comfortable and not reaching out into new potentials will surely stagnate the incredible success-mechanism we all possess, leading to boredom and apathy. In addition to not growing or expanding ourselves, we can actually withdraw or shrink our potentials as an overcompensation.

DEFENDING WHERE WE ARE

We humans have another trick that restricts us in the satisfaction game. This is our continuous tendency to logically and reasonably support and defend our current behavior. We provide plenty of reasons and good sound logic to explain why we do what we do.

I observe this daily by watching how people tend to staunchly defend the position they've taken. I frequently notice this tendency in myself, also. The problem in doing this is that it usually contains a built-in resistance to doing anything new, especially if our current behavior has been around for a long time, and even more especially if we've been avoiding something new for quite a while.

THERE IS A STRONG HUMAN TENDENCY WHEREBY WE BECOME UNWILLING TO ACKNOWLEDGE THAT THERE IS ANY VALUE IN SOMETHING THAT WE HAVE AVOIDED FOR ANY PERIOD OF TIME.

For instance, if we have avoided sitting down and writing out our goals, there will be a natural tendency to continue to avoid doing this, perhaps adding even more explanation and justification on top of why we haven't done it sooner.

If you add this tendency for us to invalidate something that we have avoided for any significant period of time to the activity to which we have already attributed a significant and *heavy* status, you might notice the resistance people have to sitting down and writing out their goals.

INVALIDATING WHERE WE ARE

An even more deeply rooted tendency is to invalidate, make wrong, put down, or otherwise make less than desirable any condition or lifestyle that we *used to be in,* one that we had previously possessed.

We tend to justify and promote our current belief, lifestyle, or behavior by comparing it favorably *over* the old way. It would appear as though the human mind has difficulty in justifying a move or transformation from condition A to condition B unless condition B is better or superior to condition A. Of course, it's quite possible that condition B is simply *different* from condition A and does not require any evaluation as to its *betterness* or *worseness* regarding condition A. Be aware of it and observe this tendency in yourself, and see how it may prevent you from moving into new things. See if it stops you from expanding into new and exciting areas in your life that could hold much satisfaction and happiness for you.

WHAT MOTIVATES US

● *The Fear of the Opposite Happening.* This is the most common form of human motivation. Most advertising is based upon fear motivation. Advertisers spend millions of dollars hourly to convince us (quite effectively, I might add) how we need their product or service so that we won't

● be left out of conversations, or be misinformed,

● be passed by our competitors, be behind the times,

● have to work harder or longer than our contemporaries,

● offend others around us,

● run out of what we need, starve, freeze, or die,

● get sick, stay sick, get worse.

● *The Incentive to Have It Happen (or The Carrot Principle).* If man cannot relate to the fear motivation (if fear of losing something does not motivate him), then incentives will almost always work. "Everybody has their price" is a common phrase. Employers encourage employees to perform by incentives such as wages and salaries, bonuses, stock options, health plans, and others. It seems that many large forward-looking companies are now at a loss to come up with any additional concepts for this form of motivation. Employees are "incentived out" and a new level of motivation seems necessary in these modern times.

● *A Genuine Desire or Want.* Aha! We've made it at last! This is the only positive motivation force. The previous two are reactions and manipulative-reactions—to fear or incentive. This form of motivation is positive—totally of your own choice. Now we can ask the person who is so together that he or she is beyond fear-motivation, beyond incentive-motivation (or The Carrot Principle), and we get down to the ultimate question:

WHAT IS IT THAT YOU REALLY WANT?

When people are no longer primarily motivated by fear or incentive, they frequently turn toward an altered attitude, a desire for improving their lifestyle, a more fulfilling life, and all those other good things.

WRITING DOWN THE REASONS

Here is where it starts getting "magical." This is where we start asking ourselves what we've been hesitant to ask. Physical rewards and incentives are nice and all that, but we've handled that department. Our basic needs seem okay for the time being, so let's look at the finer things in life.

Why haven't we done this before, you ask? Well, let us examine all the reasons why we haven't. Let us get them out of our heads and clear the way so we can get on to the exciting part. Let us examine all of the reasons why we've not listed what we wanted.

This exercise is one that I used in my Focusing Seminar and it appears to have worked really well to clear the air of any final considerations—which allows you to have more creativity and be more open with yourself when we start looking at all the things you want. Werner Erhard has observed that "People either have what they want or they have reasons why they don't have what they want." This line of Werner's seems to sum it all up for me. Whenever I notice that I don't have what I want, I see that I have some form of explanation, reason, or excuse why I don't have it.

So, take a piece of paper and a pen and make a list of every conceivable reason you have for not writing down your goals. *List them all.* Do not stop writing until you are absolutely totally certain that every consideration or reason that you have ever held in your head as an explanation for not having set goals for yourself is down on that sheet of paper.

The following examples are typical, popular with many people. If any of them work for you, copy them down and include them on your list.

EXAMPLES OF REASONS

I'm too busy.

It takes too long.

I never seem to have the time.

It seems too greedy.

I don't need a list, I can remember them.

I only have a few.

I know what I want and it's really quite simple.

That's more of that psychology stuff.

It's wrong to want things.

I don't want that much.

That's for businessmen.

I don't want to work that hard.

Yeah, I'll do that one of these days.

That's more of that motivational garbage.

That would be embarassing.

That's too silly.

Someone may find my list and read it.

I'm afraid if I write them down, I won't have any.

Oh, I don't need to do that. Everything's fine just the way it is.

They'll think I'm nuts.

Oh, man, that's heavy

Gee, that means I've go to *do* them then.

Yes, that sounds good. I think I'll do that sometime.

Take at least ten minutes on this list. It's a big one. Keep at it. When you think you have all your reasons written down, write "Any other reasons I think of later on" as the last one on the list in order to cover any one you think of after you've finished this exercise.

Now, pick up the list and crumble the paper up into a ball. Now, throw it away. Anywhere. A trash basket. The garbage can. In the incinerator. Wherever. Doesn't that feel good? All of your reasons for not having set goals before have just gone out of your life. Your mind can be clearer and more open to the concept of creating value in your life without being concerned with why you've never done it before.

Now, take another piece of paper—a clean new sheet. Make sure it is unused and has no connection with the previous piece of paper.

WRITING DOWN THE BENEFITS

We're going to make up a list of all the possible *benefits* that you could get from making up a goals list:

Don't stop writing until you have as complete a list as you can imagine. The following list may contain some possible benefits that you like. If so, copy them onto yours, but be imaginative and creative on your own.

EXAMPLES OF BENEFITS

I could actually get what I want.

It could really work.

I'll have more direction in my life.

I'll stay on purpose easier, get distracted less.

It could be a lot of fun.

It will be intriguing to see how many I have in my life.

I'll gain clarity on what I really want.

I'll even have deadlines for my goals.

I could be better able to communicate with other people on what I want.

Now, review this list again, and see if there are any reasons on this list that should be on yours. Write them all down—every possible benefit you could derive out of clearly defining what you want. Keep this list for reference and add any other benefits as you think of them. You might even use this list as a bookmark, while reading the remainder of this book.

CONDITIONING BARRIERS

Most of us have been conditioned to look at our expectations of life with an attitude that is contrary to the whole concept of setting personal goals. We have been conditioned not to expect too much. As long as we have a good home and family, what else do we need, right?

Consequently, most people have not disciplined themselves for looking at what they want. One possible exception to this is the choosing of a vocation when we are in our late high school or early college years—maybe once in our lives! We are taught *how to do* things and *how to get* along and survive, but we are not taught *how to select* what we really want—how to create our own universe the way we want it.

A common source of barriers to personal goal-setting comes out of religious misinterpretations. Almost everybody I've ever worked with in Focusing has some leftover misconceptions from their youth about their own deservingness, usually based on religious indoctrination.

People have shared with me how this comes from their childhood experiences with churches and religion, and the interpretations and decisions they made concerning the dogma and philosophies to which they were exposed.

Interestingly, it doesn't seem to be any one religion. All of them seem to have been equally misinterpreted. Consequently, there exists a lot of non-okay-ness about being truly happy, having abundance in one's life, feeling deserving and other related feelings.

I notice many people have been conditioned not to ask for things. Probably as a childhood carryover, I can see people experience much embarassment while verbalizing their goals, sharing that they are reluctant to really put their goals out there—it's like the feelings of asking for things from Santa Claus, I suppose.

"Oh, that's too silly" had been a consideration that we usually dissolved during Focusing appointments. "That's not practical." "It's too greedy to want that." "I can't expect that." These are all concepts that seem to prevent clear vision for people concerning what they really want for themselves.

When people start to state their goals, they usually begin to do so in a very cloudy, undefined manner. They really have been conditioned to be foggy about what they want. "It's safer and there is less threat if you keep it a bit vague," one middle-aged real estate broker told me. "That way, I won't be disappointed if I don't get it."

If you are vague and foggy and don't write down your goals, it may seem that you won't risk embarassment, won't risk others making fun of you, and you won't seem too greedy. It may also seem that others will like you more because you are more like them, people whom you admire and respect won't think you are weird, and that they won't think you expect too much. It may *seem* that way.

One of my own personal considerations, which has robbed me of many satisfying moments over the years, is an old conditioning pattern of always being "cool," never getting into situations where anyone would see that I was flustered or embarrassed.

While I've noticed it and observed it, and seen how it has been a barrier to my own experience of myself as well as getting in the way of a desired achievement, it still rears its head quite often. It's like a habit, so I still have to watch for it. I feel I'm way ahead of the game now, having acknowledged it, but it still hasn't disappeared completely by any means.

From my own experience, let me share how I have seen this one example of a conditioning barrier. In order to preserve "being cool" and unflustered, probably based on an extremely intelligent decision I made at a responsible age of say 9 or 10 years, I am less willing to do things that will move me along the path of my goals. If some activity needed to be done to accomplish what I wanted and it involved being "uncool," I would then avoid that activity, which would not support the achievement of my goal.

When I am getting into areas about which I am not totally familiar, such as a new business or dealing with a client in a business about which I am uninformed, it often seems uncool to ask basic questions about what is going on. I am now much more willing to admit I don't know something and to ask for the answers— not just once, but until I really get it! Sometimes this can be very embarassing, but I want to know the answers and get what I want— not be cool. Get it?

WHY CONFLICT?

There are only two explanations for conflict when you are experiencing difficulty in achieving any goal. If it seems that you really want something and you find that you just naturally keep going in the opposite direction, or you find it increasingly more frustrating, requiring more and more energy on your part to make any progress, look and see if one of the two following conditions may exist for you.

• *Question 1: Is Your Goal Really Yours?* Perhaps it's a goal or a desire you feel you *should* have. Or, it's just something very logical that your mind has decided upon for you through any number of reasonable conclusions. Could it be that you just do not desire this thing in your life enough to get yourself turned on about it? Is it just a good idea or is it truly something that supports your purpose in life? Is it your real intention or does it just sound good?

● *Question 2: Are You Willing To Do Whatever Needs To Be Done?* There is also the possibility that you really want the end result or condition to exist, but you are not willing to do what needs to be done to achieve it. It is a function of your desire to see the end result accomplished. Are you willing to do whatever needs to be done in order to see your goal realized?

So the main two questions to ask yourself if there is conflict in reaching your goals are, "Is this something I really want?" If it's quite clear that you want this, then ask yourself a second question. "Am I willing to do everything that needs to be done in order to accomplish it?"

If frustration, a sense of conflict, or any other form of problem continues to come up for you in your progression towards a goal, I would suggest looking for some lie you have told yourself regarding one of these two key questions.

NO TIME LIKE THE PRESENT

Are you ready to get on with it? Are you ready to begin doing something about how you really want your life? It may be difficult to recondition yourself. I want you to choose clearly that you want to get on with it; don't "decide" you should—"choose" to do it. Check to see that you really have the desire to get on with it, that it is not just rational logic. Be willing to take drastic action and commit yourself to creating a more satisfying life. I'll warn you that altering your point of view on several aspects of your life may be uncomfortable. Are you willing to be uncomfortable (like any other form of adventure), and receive more value from your life? Resolve yourself ("I will do it") and make that commitment to improve your life.

Benjamin Franklin said, "If you love life, do not squander time, for that is the stuff life is made of." In other words, get on with it.

Don't look back at the past—at any conditioning and blaming others or holding resentments. I want to stress here and now that in order to proceed to a more fulfilling life, you need to forget about what went on before. Unless you are writing a history book there is no value in going back. Regardless of how it may look to you, who sold you the bill of goods, whose ideas and concepts you adopted, whose principles you took on instead of your own—you bought them! You adopted them! You took them on!

You cannot go on to be absolutely responsible for the quality of your life unless you take total responsibility for it up to this point. Get this. It's important.

So, before proceeding, look at all your attitudes, beliefs, points of view, memories, and things you stand for, and see if you are blaming anyone for anything. Look and see if you are evaluating or judging anybody from your past or present life. Make sure you aren't blaming parents, relatives, children, clergy, teachers, the system, the government, your social conditions, where you lived, the "breaks," your friends, or anybody or anything. If you are blaming anyone, acknowledge that you are doing so and then you can continue.

Are you still holding onto anything or are you ready to proceed?

Theodore Roosevelt once said, "The only man who never makes a mistake is the man who never does anything!" Many people are more concerned with the possibility of making an error, a mistake, or falling short of their goal than they are with accomplishing anything of value for themselves. A mistake or an error is just that—an error. So what?! If you can't handle making a mistake, then you'd better not play—like baseball.

Not wanting to make mistakes is a very real human desire for perfection. We all make them and we can become paralyzed by the fear of making them. I've heard it said that there are two kinds of people—those who are afraid of making mistakes and those who are afraid of making mistakes *who go on and do it anyway!*

Shallow men believe in luck. Strong men believe in cause and effect.
Ralph Waldo Emerson

CHAPTER IV

MYTHS AND MISCONCEPTIONS

When I discovered how much I could contribute to the quality of my life by being really clear about what I wanted, I wondered why it was being kept such a secret.

I was given volumes and volumes of educational data in elementary school, high school, and college. I was provided with religious dogma and sense of morals. I was informed about the rules of society—the laws and the penalties for breaking them. However, the system has no provision for educating me on how to lead a satisfying life. Our culture has chosen to make the 3 R's available as basic requirements and has expanded these to the university level, including nuclear physics and calculus, literary compositions and doctoral dissertations.

Other than choosing a subject in which to major in college, which usually has a vocation attached to it, we are not encouraged, in society, to choose *the life we want.* I'm sure there are many families and even some schools which are exceptions to this generality. However, for the most part, our environment in our younger years concentrates on teaching us to read and write, getting trained for a job or career, staying out of jail, and going to Heaven.

Now, taking these objectives one at a time, let us assume that we have accomplished reading and writing. Let's say we have a job we like, or we can obtain another one that we do enjoy. Let us also assume that we have learned how to stay out of jail. Since our seat in Heaven can be presumed to be some time off yet, how do we maximize the enjoyment of this life, here on earth, the one we are experiencing right now?

The truth is that planning one's life is a relatively new concept. The human potential movement has contributed enormously to the discovery of more and more techniques that support the attaining of a higher quality of life. There is no longer any necessity to "endure" or "survive." Ultimate control over the quality of our lives is available to us right now. All you need to do is learn how to direct your life, and you begin by getting clear on just exactly how you want your life to be.

Recall any truly satisfying moments in your life and see how they corresponded to your own purposeful and conscious accomplishment of something you really wanted, a goal or self-determined end to which you were dedicated.

There are some popular myths and misconceptions that may get in the way and block the flow of personal goals. The first of these is significance.

SIGNIFICANCE

Many people feel that goals are things you set out to accomplish that are *really significant,* and therefore not to be considered for less-than-significant achievements. Common examples of "significant goals" include winning a gold medal at the Olympics, becoming the president of the United States, and sailing around the world. Other typical "significant goals" are retiring at a certain age, getting married, living in the best area in town, or becoming a vice-president of your company.

Few people recognize that some of the most valuable contributions that they could make to the quality of their own lives is to be clear about what they want, even the "insignificant" things, such as getting all those incomplete household projects done, fixing a faucet that has been dripping for two weeks, a garage that is in desperate need of spring cleaning, a worn-out needle on the home stereo phonograph. These things can really distract from the experience of being at home and truly enjoying it.

You may say, "I don't need a list to get those things done, I'll get to them soon." When are you going to do them? What do you need to do them with? What do you have to buy in order to get them done?

Little items may be just as valuable and worthy of listing as the "biggies;" they may not always have the priority that some more important things have. Some of the little items could include starting a savings account, writing those letters you've been putting off, and paying the mortgage.

There are many, many more of these "less significant items"—many more than there are of the "significant" goals. Perhaps you could see where a person could achieve his "significant goal" (say, becoming a corporate vice-president), while having little awareness of his incomplete projects at home, and wondering why he isn't feeling totally satisfied.

THINGS YOU WANT ARE THINGS YOU WANT, AND THEY DON'T NEED TO BE SIGNIFICANT OR A MAJOR PRIORITY TO BE LISTED AS GOALS!

Paul, a freelance writer, asked me for an example of one of my goals and I told him that I had just completed a very satisfying one—the replacement of several cracked window panes in my highrise apartment. He looked at me rather quizzingly and asked whether or not I thought that this kind of thing was too ordinary to be a goal.

This is an example of where you need to be your own judge of what's important to you! In my case, the cracked windows had been a confrontation for me for several months. I live in a Russian Hill highrise in San Francisco with a view I consider incomparable. The distraction caused by the cracked windows, the amount of negotiating and prodding to get them repaired, and the time period that was necessary made this "ordinary" activity significant enough for me to include on my goals list.

Quite often, these seemingly little things have more to do with our well-being than the ones we put out as our "biggies" anyway. Priorities may vary, but anything you want is worthy of being listed. Sometimes the things we consider the most important are buried deep and would never be included on a list.

SCARCITY

Another common misconception about "goals" is that you can only have a limited number of them. Many people act as if there is a rationing of goals, and each person is only allowed a predetermined number in his or her lifetime.

I have often heard a person say, "Oh, yes, I had a goal once—to become a teacher," or, "Well, I have two goals: to retire in a year's time and to sail around the world in my own boat." A very common idea is that we need to have "a" goal, and many people cherish their single "goal" like a prized trophy. In fact, many people have shared with me how they are worried about accomplishing their single goal and fear that there will be nothing left for them.

I am not suggesting that you should have lots of goals, but many people feel that one or two is all that they are allowed!

THERE IS NO SCARCITY OF GOALS!

Literally nothing would get done on this planet without someone wanting it to happen. Every action requires an intention, albeit often unexpressed or uncommunicated. Thousands of "goals" are achieved every minute on this earth.

In working with individuals in goal-setting, I'd estimate the average person discovers forty to one hundred goals he or she wants to list. It is my theory that these are only the tip of the iceberg. We have wants and desires for nearly every area of our lives, so why not express them?

Quite frequently, when someone discovers that I am an enthusiastic goal-setting advocate, they will inform me of *Their Goal* (as if they had just *one*) as if they have already achieved goal-setting perfection (when they have really only just begun). They see the value in setting goals but are still confined or limited by accepting the concept of scarcity or a shortage of the supply available to them.

GREED

One of the most common blocks or barriers to people expressing their wants (often on a below-conscious level) is an idea that expressing one's desires is wrong, sinful, or otherwise socially unacceptable. For many people, concepts of greed and other unattractive conceptualizations prevent them from allowing themselves to acknowledge that they truly want something. It seems to be similar to admitting having a sexual thought about somebody and being too embarassed to admit it to yourself. There is some shame and guilt attached even to the simple admission of it sometimes.

One of the most often expressed feelings I heard from people during Focusing appointments went something like, "John, I don't want much—just to be happy." One woman hesitantly expressed this sentiment as if that one goal might be considered "wanting too much" by other people.

DENYING WHAT YOU WANT AND PRETENDING IT DOESN'T EXIST DOES NOT SERVE YOUR LIFE AT ALL!

Perhaps due to misconceptions with regard to religious training in our childhood, many of us have experienced some conflict between personally wanting something and a picture of wrongness about wanting that thing. We might tend to persecute ourselves for wanting it because "no really good person would want that." Let me be clear that I am not talking about immoral or unethical things, or criminal acts; I am talking about simple ethical goals, such as wanting a large New York steak at a very deluxe restaurant (when somewhere else in the world someone might be starving and your guilt prevents you from expressing that goal).

It took me quite some time to acknowledge that I really enjoyed food and eating and finally got rid of the picture I had of starving people in Europe (from my childhood) whenever I ate a meal. I had that drummed into my head for years and the conditioning that I was holding was actually diminishing my experience of eating.

DRUDGERY—NO FUN

A frequently expressed idea about setting goals is that great amounts of unrewarding effort will be required in order to achieve the goal. Many people refrain from setting any kind of goal due to this preconceived notion.

I have observed that when you are doing something that you really want to do, it is an exhilarating experience. Doing something that you don't want to do *can* be a drudgery, indeed!

THIS IS WHERE CLARITY AND CERTAINTY ABOUT WHAT YOU WANT IS A FANTASTIC ASSET!

"CONCRETE" GOALS

When you are really certain about a goal, dedication, commitment, and all the activities that support the accomplishment of that
goal all flow very naturally and effortlessly. It's fun, energizing and
extremely satisfying!

On the other hand, when you doubt if you want your goal, or
have no conscious goal, the same activity, commitment, and
dedication can be very exhausting and unrewarding, often being a
struggle requiring large amounts of effort and *certainly* no fun! This
often results when the goal is really just a good idea—made up in
order to have a goal.

FEAR OF FAILURE

Another barrier to many people—a block or obstacle that
seems to interfere with making a commitment to have something
happen—is an often-unconscious fear of failure if it doesn't happen. Our society seems to have created a very negative concep-
tualization of a "failure," to the point that many people don't try
anything, rather than confronting the possibility of failure.

You have absolute total choice on how you evaluate a failed
goal. You can make it as significant as you like or you can look at a
failed goal as it really is—a missed target, or a mistake. When you
fall short of the goal, you do not need to feel like a "failure,"
bringing up all the pictures, memories, and concepts you have
about failures. For example, if you didn't become a vice-president
by the date you had targeted, you need not picture yourself as the
Harold Stassen of the business world. It's okay to feel some sad-
ness or discontent, but be responsible for how you treat yourself.

ONLY FOR BUSINESS

A popular opinion is that goal-setting is only for careers or the
business community—the professionals. Getting really clear on
what you want is certainly a professional approach to living, I agree.
I would like to live life professionally, too. Wouldn't you? When it
comes down to the quality and the degree of satisfaction you
experience in your life, who wants to be an amateur?

Business executives who live every day in goal-oriented positions at work still resist applying the same principles to their personal lives, often creating an imbalance among their personal, social, career, and psychological desires and wants.

ONLY FOR SPORTS

Another popular concept is that goals are targets that athletes set for top performance. Physical performances, dexterity, scoring skill, muscle power, and agility goals are very short-term goals and therefore satisfy our impatient appetite for immediate results.

Many people look at goal-setting as only for athletes (in terms of physical prowess or ability) and not for people who are not engaged in sports-oriented activities. Even our vocabulary supports this idea, given that "goals" are identified with several organized sports, such as football, hockey, basketball, and soccer.

STRAIN AND EFFORT

Perhaps due to the business and sports connotation given to the subject of goals by so many people, another misconception is that goal-setting requires a lot of effort and strain. Ironically, experienced goal-setters report that they are energized by the clarity that they experience, the single-mindedness of their purpose, and the clear understanding of where they are going. They report "less effort than doing nothing at all!"

A goal is a future desired condition. That future can be the next minute or the next century. Setting a goal is simply determining where you want to be and when you want to be there. Everything about you is the result of a goal you set—perhaps unconsciously, perhaps not verbally or written down, but, nevertheless, a goal.

DESERVINGNESS

For most people, the biggest single block to getting really clear on what they want (the first step to getting what they want) is a subconscious doubt or earlier decision about their deservingness.

Are you willing to have what you want? Will you feel really good when you get it? Do you deserve to have it? Are you sure you'll allow yourself to accomplish what you want to or will you come up with a way to sabotage your success? Sabotage is very common, by the way, so don't feel odd if you have noticed this pattern in your past accomplishments.

CONDITIONING

We humans do pick up attitudes and habits and ideas along the road of life. We make decisions every day that are based on habit and preconceived notions that we adopted from people and events in our past environments.

You can read about our conditioning, its influences, and how it controls our every-day behavior in (any of the) many books on psychology, motivation, and behavioral sciences. You can begin to look at what conditioning concepts you may have running your life right now. *Everybody* has preconceived notions and attitudes, not just a few people. The only possible exceptions would be those who were raised in test tubes, under ideal laboratory conditions, and (as we've already read) they have most likely perished anyway.

Going to the moon isn't very far; the greatest distance we have to cover still lies within us.

Charles de Gaulle

CHAPTER V

THE VALUE OF WRITTEN GOALS

I feel very strongly about the value to be found in writing down your wants and desires. Some people feel overwhelmed or uneasy about writing down everything they want. They just think about it a lot. Somehow it seems that there is just too much to consider and comprehend; they get "reasonable" about it—discrediting their real, true desires. *Thinking* about what is wanted in life is one of our favorite pastimes, *and* nothing gets done! It also uses up great amounts of energy that we could be using to produce some positive results.

WRITING DOWN YOUR DESIRES IS THE SINGLE MOST VALUABLE ACTION YOU CAN TAKE TO ACCOMPLISH WHAT YOU WANT!

Alan Lakein writes, ". . . Thinking about your goals is usually quite a different experience from writing them down. Unwritten goals often remain vague or utopian dreams, such as 'travel' or 'becoming a millionaire.' Writing goals down tends to make them more concrete and specific and helps you to go below the surface of the same old cliches you've been telling yourself for years."

RESISTANCE

Your mind has a tendency to keep *thinking about* what you want and resist the idea of sitting down and writing it all out. I cannot explain the reasons for this phenomenon, but I certainly can observe it in nearly everyone, including myself.

This resistance needs to be acknowledged. If you are one of those who has looked at doing this before and feel that you fall into this category (being resistant to writing down what you want in your life), acknowledge that you've done this—*acknowledge your resistance*. Don't try to deny it. Denying it will add to the likelihood of its staying there, getting in the way.

So acknowledge your resistance if you feel you have any. In fact, acknowledge your resistance even if you aren't aware of it. I've developed the technique of Focusing by recognizing this resistance, assisting people who continually wanted to put it off, change the topic of conversation, postpone it to a later date, etc.

THE RUBBERBAND THEORY

My Rubberband Theory consists of the concept that our innermost desires tend to stay buried, back in our "unconscious" (not our "subconscious"), and our minds seem to prefer keeping them there so we can think about them often. Since we are going to drag them out and look at them all to get a good, clear picture of what we really want for ourselves, why not write them down?

Since we've conquered all the resistance of doing it and we've finally put some conscious attention on these wants, let's write them down so we don't have to go through this again. Why go through this whenever we want some clarity? All of our wants and desires will retreat back into our minds after we've written them down. They aren't going to be tattooed on our foreheads, you know. Writing down our wants and desires is similar to taking a picture of them before they can leave us, returning to our unconscious.

Writing down your goals makes them very real and concrete. The writing of your goals demonstrates to the physical universe that you are serious about them and that these are truly things you want in your life. The act itself is a form of commitment on your part—a demonstration of your willingness to have these things in your life.

Once these goals are etched on paper, written down, and preserved in print, they will remain real for you even though your mind may revert to "reasonable explanations" of how silly they were, how ashamed you should be for wanting them, and all of the other conditioned nonsense that your mind may create for you in order to explain why you've never made a comprehensive list of what you want.

While your desires for yourself may leave your day-in day-out awareness, you will have preserved them in a very real way that will serve you in having them happen.

Something very "magical" happens when it comes to written goals. Very often, goals are achieved, attained, or accomplished without any conscious action on the part of the goal-setter, other than simply listing them. Many motivational experts agree that half of the job is done in terms of achieving a given objective when that objective is expressed in a written form!

IMAGINE THAT—WRITING DOWN YOUR GOALS CAN GET YOU HALFWAY TOWARDS ACCOMPLISHING THEM!

Jeff, an attorney, wrote out a list of about a dozen 6-month goals for himself and, ironically, promptly lost them. Six months later, he discovered his list. He was utterly amazed to discover that each and every one of his wants and desires, as expressed on his list, had materialized! He was not aware of having done anything and yet they had all come to pass over the half year that the list was lost.

MIRACLE LIST

Marcia calls her goals list her "miracle list." She keeps it stored away, and takes it out every now and then to review it, checking off her miracles and adding new "miracles" she would like in her life. She reports nearly absolute success with all her miracles. It has become very matter-of-fact for her now and she has been doing this for several years.

Consciously, that is all the effort or energy she spends on it! Marcia reviews her list once or twice a year and she is very pleased with the results. "It used to blow my mind," she told me one day, "but now I see that these fantastic results are just another part of my life."

DO WHATEVER WORKS

If you would prefer to refer to your goals as "miracles," then I heartily suggest you do so. Do whatever works for you. Have fun with the entire process. There is a "magic" about this whole game called life, or living, so enjoy it more and don't be terribly concerned about understanding how it works.

HIGHLIGHTS IN YOUR LIFE

The ultimate proof of how rewarding life can be, when you set out to do something and are conscious of attaining it, can be dramatized by looking back on the most satisfying moments in your life.

Take a piece of paper and list all of the really memorable moments in your life, when you really felt whole and satisfied, with a sense of purpose and direction. Start with when you were a child and work yourself up to the present day. Really now, take about fifteen minutes and make a list. Keep writing as long as things are coming up and recollections are there for you.

TAKE A FULL FIFTEEN MINUTES TO REVIEW YOUR LIFE.

Were these moments the result of accomplished goals you had set for yourself, even if not in writing? Were these the times when something came out just the way you wanted it to? When you met someone you really wanted to meet? When you designed or figured out something you had been working on for some time?

Now, keep looking and notice the relationship between the degree of difficulty, or uncertainty, that you had about doing them and the quality of the feeling you had at the time of their accomplishment or attainment.

Did you discover something about your own ability? Did you feel more able? Did you feel you found a new talent within yourself? Did you feel that you really made a contribution to someone else's life?

62

Notice the relationship between the satisfaction you experienced and the degree to which the results were *exactly* as you wanted them. See how good you felt when what you did or accomplished was your very own idea, and not somebody else's.

A SENSE OF DIRECTION: CERTAINTY

I have observed that people who discover what they want seem to have richer, fuller lives. As a result of being clearer about what they want, they gain more control over their lives, reacting less like "victims" of life. They become self-assured and find hidden energies within themselves.

These same people find a new sense of certainty that we all seem to like to have about us, knowing where we are going. Can you imagine getting into your car and not knowing where you are going, or if you know your destination, not knowing what route you're going to take? We tend to like certainty in our lives—we like to know where we are going when we get into the car.

Discovering your goals has the effect of moving you into the driver's seat. Instead of being a passenger and just going along for the ride, wherever the driver is headed, you now are making the decisions, choosing the route, making the turns, keeping on schedule—knowing where you are going and what time you want to be there.

Isn't it more fun to be involved in the planning of the trip and active instead of being a passive passenger?

You can now begin to see your role as a "cause" in your life in the quality you experience in your day-to-day living. It will seem that your life is less like the result or "effect" of some outside force such as society, the family, the job, or some other power outside of you. Your life can have direction and purpose—those great mystical and elusive characteristics that poets write about, that songwriters compose ballads about, and that philosophers philosophize about. You can become a self-determined individual!

By discovering your own personal goals you will become more open to a wide range of positive experiences, based on what others have reported publicly or shared with me privately. The majority of people who have completed the Focusing process report that they have more certainty about what's ahead for them, with many of them feeling a tremendously increased sense of purpose as well. Of those persons who stay in touch with me, I hear they feel more in control of their lives, spending less time bogged down in unsatisfying situations. A higher quality of life has been unanimously reported by all Focusing clients as is an experience of higher energy and increased enthusiasm.

STARTING THE DAY

I have noticed that when I have projects, meetings, trips, appointments, or plans for any specific activity, I wake up more eagerly, feel much more energized in the morning and, generally, I experience much more excitement about the challenge of the day.

On those days when I have no specific plans or activities I am planning, such as when I simply set aside a day to work on a project without any specific objectives, I notice that I get out of bed with much less enthusiasm. Comparatively, I feel more apathetic, with kind of a ho-hum attitude. On some occasions I'll reset the alarm and sleep a little longer—a behavior that certainly does not support much aliveness.

While these kinds of days are more and more rare in my life, they are reminiscent of days gone by, when they occurred with much more frequency.

Personally, I have found that the attitude that I have on awakening in the morning has a tremendous influence on how my day progresses, which makes a much larger contribution to my week, which, of course, makes an even bigger contribution to my month, which has an enormous influence over my year, which has a significant bearing on my entire life!

If your intention is to engage in some satisfying activity and you have some plans for the day, observe the level of excitement you experience upon awakening. If you work for someone else, watch the difference in how you arise in the morning when you are simply going to the job because you are paid to be there, as compared to when you have a project you have personally become involved in.

Your attitude upon getting up each day is definitely related to your goals, your plans for the day, the projects that are important to you. This applies whether you are employed and working on a job, a student attending school, or simply pursuing personal pleasures each day on your own.

THE SPIRAL EFFECT

There is a fantastic spiral effect in setting goals, once you've become initiated. After you start maintaining your goals, monitoring them, and setting new goals, you will become more and more willing to acknowledge things that you want in your life.Once the gate has been opened and you realize that you've survived the experience you will tend to let more and more out.

Once you've "played" with goals for awhile, recognized the value and observed how good it feels, once you've become more comfortable with the process, you will start to look deeper into what you really want, what kind of person you want to be, what you want to do, and want to have, both in the short term and for the long-range future. The time that this takes and the degree of discomfort to be experienced will vary from person to person. Some people retreat back inside and slam the gate! However, for those who keep opening the valve and making the commitment to participate, there are unlimited rewards!

For example, when I first started listing my goals, I had seventeen of them on my list. In less than one year I had increased my list to include nearly one hundred fifty! I found that the valve had just opened and it flowed more easily each time.

In addition to the exposure of deeper-set desires, the spiral effect also demonstrates itself in terms of more and more challenging desires. As you begin accomplishing, attaining, and achieving what you want, you tend to set higher and higher goals, feeling more and more confident. Again, this is man's nature—to keep seeking his maximum potential. But it is not like someone is forcing you to set these goals. They are all your own idea—they are yours! To outside observers, your friends, or others who see the results in your life, your accomplishments may seem to get more and more outstanding and exceptional, depending upon whether or not you keep following one path or keep starting new ones each time.

Can you imagine how exciting it can be (as you are becoming more and more experienced at goal-setting), enjoying the continuous discovery of desires within yourself, simultaneously seeking higher and more challenging levels on which to play? This spiraling effect is kinetic, constantly expanding, with no bounds whatsoever!

Just imagine how exciting and energizing life can be when you are continuously expanding the level of the game you are playing.

All the benefits of discovering your goals are multiplied continuously. Your willingness to be in total control of your life is enhanced. Your self-assurance increases each day. Your level of participation expands constantly. You are increasingly more willing to share yourself, to receive support from others, to have more and more value in your experience of every-day living. You will be less restrained in communicating, due to increased self-confidence.

You will be having more and more fun, feeling more and more energized—NOT BECAUSE YOU FEEL YOU SHOULD OR YOU HAVE TO, BUT BECAUSE YOU *WANT* TO!

The fabulous story of *Jonathan Livingston Seagull,* by Richard Bach, is a beautiful illustration of this behavioral pattern in our society. Jonathan Livingston Seagull dared to be outstanding and set new goals for himself. He blew the minds of the seagull community! He dared to do things and have feelings that other seagulls had blocked themselves from having.

Finally, in looking at the rewards that can be yours through goal-setting, I want to stress that you can always have fun with your goals! Your goals are agreements that you make with yourself. It is possible to pursue goals with a light heart and with an attitude of pure joy.

How much more there is to living! Instead of our drab slogging forth and back to the fishing boats, there's a reason to life! We can lift ourselves out of ignorance, we can find ourselves as creatures of excellence and intelligence and skill. We can be free! We can learn to fly!

Richard Bach
Jonathan Livingston Seagull

CHAPTER VI

A GUARANTEE

Through my own experience, I have witnessed nearly all of my Focusing clients become much more joyful and communicative in their endeavors after getting clearer about what they wanted. Invariably, each person with whom I still have any contact is more individualistic than they were before, less restrained by self-imposed limitations than they were before listing their goals.

Their eyes even seem clearer and there seems to be little wasted energy—making them much more effective. They are much more willing to support others, a common occurrence when people feel really good about themselves.

I have also observed much more willingness on their parts to have things, to receive support, to own things, to be famous, to go on outrageous trips, etc.

When I meet new people who already demonstrate any of these characteristics, I invariably discover that they are already veteran goal-setters, perhaps not to the degree of detail we will be going for here in this book, but, nevertheless, goal-oriented people. Some of these people don't even consider themselves as such, because they just do it automatically. To them, clarity and knowing what they want is a very natural part of their lives. A majority of people, however, can find tremendous value in dissolving the barriers to being clear, naturally.

PROMISES

When you have completed the Focusing process, I *promise* that the quality of your life, and the degree of satisfaction you will experience in your day-to-day living, will increase dramatically!

I *promise* you that you will begin discovering more and more about yourself and you will feel more energized and purposeful. I *promise* that you will feel more certain, more adventurous, and more excited about where your life is leading. If you continue to tend your goals, updating, correcting, and adjusting them as conditions change in your life and in the world around you, I'll further *guarantee* you that this natural high will continue for as long as you keep it up. Your life will always contain highs and lows, peaks and valleys, times when you are on top of the world, and times when you wonder what is going on. That's how the game is played since we need "lows" to have "highs." But if you are always willing to go for what you really want, starting with being clear about what you are going for, I guarantee your highs will be higher, your lows will be higher, and you'll spend more time—more of your lifetime—in "highness" than in "lowness."

COMPETENCE

There are some theories that each person has a level of competence beyond which he or she cannot rise. These theories are based on a finite requirement for certain abilities seeking out a compatible *filler* for that need, representing the needed ability. Dr. Lawrence Peter's famous Peter Principle states that, "In a hierarchy, every employee tends to rise to his level of incompetence." I would like to suggest a modification of Dr. Peter's theory—that people tend to rise to a level of ability or competence above which they *think* they can no longer rise. Their competence does not stop them—only their belief that they are incompetent.

YOU ARE ONLY LIMITED BY WHAT YOUR MIND HAS DECIDED YOUR LIMITS WILL BE.

If you have made a decision that you could never accomplish something, you can try all you want and you'll never accomplish it. You have already set the limit.

For instance, if you have decided that your marriage has to have some problems in it, because that's the way life is, you will never allow yourself to have a trouble-free marriage. You will subconsciously create problems whenever it looks too good.

In our Focusing session, Maria discovered that she had imposed drastic limitations on herself by holding onto a concept that in order to set a goal for herself, she needed to know how to get to it, how it was to be accomplished. She thought that unless she knew how to do it, she couldn't think of it as a real objective.

One of the realizations that she had in the session was that the world was full of people who can do things for her, and that all she needed to do was get clear about her intention to have her goal, regardless of whether or not she knew how she'd get it.

Start looking at how you limit yourself. See how your own decisions about how things are supposed to be may be limiting your ability to have certain things in your life. Notice how many things you have seen as unattainable, that you've prevented yourself from getting. See how you may have predetermined what you could have and what you could not have.

Mastering life is the process of moving from where you are to where you want to be.

Werner Erhard

CHAPTER VII

THE FOCUSING PRINCIPLE

The principle of Focusing is to break down and subdivide all typical areas of your life in order for you to look at each one individually and *focus* on it, in order to closely examine what you want for yourself in that particular area of your life.

Recognizing that we all have very distinct and different ideas of what we want and when we want them to become real for us, we will be looking at any and all conditions that you want in your life.

There are no suggestions concerning what your wants *should* be or deadlines for when you *should* want them. The categories are meant to trigger desires you've been suppressing in that area, not to promote goals that aren't there. You are the composite of what you want to be, do, and have. Your desires and wants are an integral part of who you are.

The desires that you express are the sum total of how you want your life to be. We are not out to make up or manufacture any goals or desires. We want to get at what your real intentions are. Be thinking of how you want your life to be; what kind of experience of yourself do you want. What do you want to do; what things do you want to have?

BE, DO, AND HAVE

Be, do, and have. Keep these three words in the forefront of your mind throughout this exercise. Many people look only at the "things" they want, or the activities or "doing" part of life. By keeping these three verbs in your consciousness throughout the exercises, you will be reminding yourself of *all* the facets of yourself, especially the "being" part, from which everything else comes!

THE FOCUSING PRINCIPLE

YOU, OTHERS, AND THE UNIVERSE

The categories we will be covering have been divided into three primary subdivisions. This allows you to keep your attention on one point of view throughout each subdivision, allowing most of your energy to be focused on looking at what you want.

These three subdivisions are:

- WHAT YOU WANT FOR YOUR EXPERIENCE OF YOURSELF;

- WHAT YOU WANT REGARDING YOUR INTERACTION WITH OTHERS;

- WHAT THINGS YOU WANT FROM THE PHYSICAL UNIVERSE.

By going through each of these areas, one at a time, you will be better able to concentrate on all the suggested categories, with an overview of the main subdivision.

Utilizing the Focusing principle, many people have found it much easier to look at what they want. The whole process becomes much more appetizing and appears much less overwhelming. Focusing also exists as a form or structure within which you can commit yourself to complete the looking experience. It's like playing an entire ballgame, with a *beginning,* a *middle,* and an *end,* rather than going out on the street and throwing a ball around until dinnertime—a perennial *middle.*

Bob, a California realtor, had spent several years "thinking about" leaving the family business, a second-generation real estate brokerage. In one of the earliest Focusing seminars, he chose to quit thinking about it; he chose to leave the business after seven years; he also chose to select a plan of action that included his own personal goals. Within one year, he had developed his own company and had established partial ownership in two other real estate-related companies.

THE GUIDELINES

Focusing utilizes basic guidelines that work very well for people in recognizing what they want. I've used these guidelines myself and I have found them to be extremely valuable, for my own goals and in my work with others in setting their initial goals and also in maintaining goals once they have been listed. Even as an experienced goal-setter, I will still occasionally catch an omission in checking over my own goal list by using these guidelines.

- "OWN" YOUR OWN GOAL.

- BE WILLING FOR IT TO HAPPEN.

- SEE IT AS ATTAINABLE.

- INTEND IT TO HAPPEN.

- WRITE: EXACTLY WHAT YOU WANT.

- WRITE: EXACTLY WHEN YOU WANT IT.

- WRITE: IN A POSITIVE LANGUAGE.

- WRITE: AS IF IT EXISTS NOW.

- *"Own" Your Goal.* The goals you set must be your very own! This may sound like an unnecessary or very obvious prerequisite and you may wonder why I've included it here.

IT HAS BEEN MY EXPERIENCE THAT A MAJOR SOURCE OF DISSATISFACTION EXPERIENCED BY MANY PEOPLE IS THAT THEY ARE NOT ACHIEVING THE GOALS THAT *THEY* REALLY WANT!

These people, even though they are fantastic achievers and very effective individuals, were striving for goals they felt they "should" have—things they were impressed with as being what they should work for in their lives.

Sound crazy? You bet it is. However, many people are very busy striving for goals they've set without really personally *owning* them or taking personal responsibility for them.

Decisions you made as a child or in your early adult years could easily be influencing what you are now doing or feel you should be doing. The most common mistake is where people set goals which they feel they "should" set and are, therefore, seeking goals that they think someone else wants them to achieve.

An example of this kind of behavior could easily be the person who is continuously struggling to get rich but has never really given much thought as to whether he or she really *wants* to be rich.

A very common example of a non-owned goal is the concept of early retirement. Many people work and plan their lives in order to retire early—the Great American Dream. Seldom, however, is this retirement satisfactory. It usually results in either a depressed regression of the individual, sometimes resulting in a shorter life, or a new activity altogether.

Working towards a goal that someone else thinks you ought to achieve is not a very satisfying endeavor. Desire falls off sharply when you are just doing something because you think you should or it is the "right thing to do."

Recognizing whether or not your goals are really yours (not some good idea you picked up from your family or peers) is one of the most difficult parts of goal-setting. I have noticed that this area is where most people experience uncertainty about what they really want.

A simple test for whether or not your goal is really yours is to see how much it "turns you on." Are you excited about the possibility of attaining it? Do you feel a "rush" when you think about it or is it just your mind telling you that this is the kind of thing you "should" want in order to conform to some ideal picture of yourself?

Mimi, a real estate saleswoman, was telling me how many "goals" she had written down. Her problem, she explained to me, was getting to them. It appeared that her "goals" or the activities she had listed might not really be what she wanted since she had difficulty getting around to doing them. This is another test to see if you really want something—want it enough to stay excited about doing it.

Set your goals with the imagination of a child, but list them as an adult. Plan your goals with deadlines for their achievement and stages of accomplishment all planned out, as an intelligent adult; but, look at what you want as a child who has very few limitations on his or her imagination. Be creative, imaginative, and true to your own desires. Children have not yet been sold a bill of goods that serve as barriers to a totally self-fulfilled life. Did you ever notice how easily children get what they want?

Many people do the exact opposite—setting goals with their minds, using the powers of reason, logic, and rational thinking, and then act like children planning how they are going to accomplish them. They keep their goals in their heads, vague and cloudy, and allow every activity around them to distract them.

Your own goals need to be totally ethical for you to enjoy achievement and satisfaction. Your ethics are the criteria, not someone else's "good idea." You need to be absolutely ethical—true to your standards and morals for your goals to work. To be true to someone else's ethics is "unethical," a lie, and will sabotage your satisfaction—the goals you set will be somebody else's.

Gary told me how much he wanted to start reading regularly, but he "never had the time." When I pressured him to keep looking at this goal, he realized he felt that he *should* read more and that he actually had no interest in reading! As a result of this realization, he was freed of this conflict and could relax and really enjoy "not reading!" By owning your goals you can rid yourself of any needless items you are carrying around in your head which you don't really want—you just think you want. These "unwanted" goals are examples of wasted energy and needless baggage for you to be carrying around.

● *Be Willing For It To Happen.* Picture yourself in, or with, the condition you want; see yourself being the kind of person you want to be, doing the things you want to do, having what you are expressing you want to have. Visualize the result; make certain you will have the result you desire. Imagine the *exact feeling* you will experience when you have reached your goal.

Does it fit? Are you willing to have it realized? Are you desirous of this goal becoming a reality or do you want to keep it as a dream?

Do you have any problem with your deservingness to have this goal realized? Are you afraid that there may not be enough of what you want? Are you concerned that if this goal is actually realized, there may be nothing left for you in the future?

If you are not absolutely certain that you are willing for your goal to become a reality, then it is a waste of time and energy on your part to even consider it as something to have on your goal list (unless the purpose is to simply have another item on your list).

I often wonder how willing people are to have their wants and desires realized when they steadfastly refuse to list what they want. They seemingly would rather remain muddled and unclear than to be clear and organized about that which they want. This seems to be an indication of *unwillingness* to have their goals realized.

Playboy magazine once published a cartoon that was very appropriate to the subject of "wanting, but unwilling to have." While God was parting the waters of the Red Sea, miraculously exposing a wide corridor to the Promised Land, a figure, who appeared to be Moses, was complaining to the heavens, "But we'll get our sandals all muddy!" This seems like a near-perfect example of how someone can be so unwilling to have a miracle performed on their behalf that they need to find fault with the way it was done.

I've seen numerous occasions when people found frustration and dissatisfaction working towards a predetermined goal only to discover that they were unconsciously sabotaging their progress, based upon their unwillingness to actually have it become a reality.

Who was it who said, "Be careful of what you want in life, you may get it"?

● *See It As Attainable.* You need to see your goals as being attainable for yourself. Don't set your goals so high that you can't see any chance of their becoming real. It doesn't matter if others can't see them as attainable, as long as *you* can! If you don't see any way you can make it, you are just setting yourself up to lose at the goal-setting game. I see no way to provide guidelines for what is attainable for you; it is very personal and only you know how you feel about it.

Personally, I don't think we are capable of true desire for a condition to exist in our lives unless we possess the ability to attain it. Sometimes we set ourselves up to lose, by setting unattainable goals—but then this is not *real* desire—it is manufactured by considerations of what we think we *should* have.

Don't get trapped by going for goals that you "think" are attainable, based on the "everything is possible" theorem or belief. If you cannot see your goal as really attainable, for *you,* don't set it for yourself. We all have different personal realities and we have to be consistent with our *own* realities. What is considered possible by one person will not necessarily be considered as possible by another. Don't buy someone else's idea of reality!

Personally, I don't spend time worrying about whether a desire of mine is unattainable. If I really want it, I know I am capable of attaining it. Discovering new capabilities in myself is a part of the fun and excitement of it all. This is my own personal approach and I certainly don't recommend you take it unless you agree totally with the concept.

If you don't happen to agree with me and would rather trust your own intellectual assessment of your capability to attain it, that's fine, too. Whatever you do, don't set yourself up to lose! Your mind has to see that you *can* achieve the desired end that you designate.

Whatever you see as real and challenging—yet possible— makes for a good goal-setting subject. To set a goal that you dream about, but hold in a framework called "impossibility," or "I'll never get that," or any other similar negative context, is foolish and unsupportive of your own well-being.

Jim is an engineer who has spent several years in the pursuit of expanding his consciousness and awareness. His goal might seem impossible to many people's standards and yet it is totally attainable from where he sits.

In a moment of looking quietly at decisions he had made in his life, Jim discovered a decision he made at the age of nine, while living in Arkansas. He decided that he had poor eyesight and subsequently developed such poor eyesight as to prove himself blind. He couldn't even read the large E at the top of most charts used for testing.

Preparing to leave San Francisco for a trip to India, Jim shared with me how he was progressing toward the elimination of his need to wear glasses. His goal was to achieve an ability to see without corrective lenses of any kind—a rather dramatic objective by most people's point of view. However, his reality was such that he saw it as being *very attainable,* even though extremely challenging.

He was using corrective contact lenses and had achieved 20/50 vision in the few months he had been working at it. At the age of 30, Jim was using the same intention to reverse his childhood decision, changing from a decision "not to see" to a decision "to see perfectly."

Be willing to take some risks! Adventure is what makes life exciting! Tax your confidence in yourself and allow a little uncertainty (about whether or not you can really do it) to enter into the picture. Allow just enough uncertainty to exist to excite you into doing what you want to do. No one said that it would not be difficult to achieve the desired results you wish. Life is not necessarily about things being comfortable and easy, as we've seen in the preceeding pages.

• *Intend It To Happen.* Your intention is the ultimate power in the universe. It is the source of all your energy to effect an accomplishment—to make something happen that you want to have happen.

To demonstrate the power of intention, the power of our ability to manifest "miracles" in our day-to-day living, I could cite hundreds and hundreds of personal observations, as well as recalling incidents shared by others. One situation in particular comes to mind, however.

David, a beautiful man who, at the time, was a practicing dentist, shared a story with me that I feel compelled to include here. While in South America, he was guided deep into the jungle country, traveling by cross-country vehicles in a convoy. It was a long hot trek and, while he enjoyed the trip in, he was not looking forward to the return trip to civilization. He began to fantasize as how he might return to civilization more comfortably.

Near their destination, he observed the traces of an old airfield. When he inquired about it, he was informed that planes no longer used the airstrip—it had been abandoned years before. He insisted on driving closer and inspecting the airfield, much to the impatience and opposition of his local guides and the rest of his party. While he was checking out the old airport, the drone of an airplane's engine came into earshot.

David recalled how a small commercial aircraft landed while his party watched in awe. The pilot informed him that he needed to land in order to repair a simple mechanical problem. Once the crew had repaired the plane, the pilot informed David that he'd be pleased to give him a lift, since the plane was headed for the same destination as he was.

The bottom line—David wanted to fly out of the jungle rather than return by the overland route. A nonscheduled plane lands at the abandoned airfield, headed for the same destination, and has space available for an extra passenger. David wanted to fly back and he got to fly back! Additionally, I'd like you to know that David's personal reality allows for "miracles" such as this. In other words, it was not all that "unreasonable" for David to create an airplane landing in the middle of the jungle. His own reality incorporated these kinds of incredible and "unbelievable" incidents.

Do you intend to improve the quality of your life? Do you intend to get as much satisfaction out of living as you can?

Do you honestly intend to have the things that you will be writing down soon? If what you want takes courage and risk, are you willing to take the risk? Do you have the courage? If not, can you develop your courage in order to allow you to get what you want?

I suggest that you look at goals as the words expressing your intention, not as "things I'd *like* to have."

Sure, I'd *like* to have a private executive Lear jet, a full-time crew, and all the money to maintain it. It would be nice, I am sure. However, I don't seriously *intend* to have it in my life. I have no energy or power behind the desire—it would be nice, but that's all.

Without intention, there is no determination, no desirous attitude, no real *will* for it!

The Random House College Dictionary defines intent as "having the attention sharply fixed upon something; determined; having the mind or will fixed on some purpose or goal."

This element is probably the most frequently missing ingredient in people's lives. They may be able to state a few things they'd like, but there is absolutely no intention behind the statements—words alone don't do it!

Conversely, many have an intention of which they are hardly aware—to conform to the same lifestyle and ambition of all their peers and contemporaries. Guess what? They get it. And then they wonder what's missing in their lives!

See if you trust yourself to follow through on your goal. Are you trustworthy to deliver the goods? If you were observing yourself, would you trust the level of interest you possess? If you were your own boss, would you feel confident that you would do the job?

So, make certain that the things you will be stating and writing down are things you *intend* to have in your life.

● *Write It Down: Exactly What You Want.* Writing down your goals is a commitment to the world; you have put your goal out into the physical universe when you write it down on paper. Written goals show that you are serious about them and that you have progressed beyond the "hoping it will all work out" level. Writing down what you want is the most crucial first step you can take towards *reaching* your goals.

Whenever there is any doubt as to whether or not you should write down a goal, whenever you aren't quite sure if you should write it down or not, go ahead. After all, what is the cost to you?

Why not write it down? What harm could it possibly do? Weigh the possible benefits against the possible detriments.

Written goals serve to keep you thinking about what you want—your mind will unconsciously do what needs to be done in order to achieve it. And it usually happens automatically and without any conscious effort.

Considering the enormous quantities of goals that the average person can author, I find it inconceivable that anyone, no matter how intelligent, can keep a very clear picture of what they want in their heads.Most people seem to hibernate with vague concepts of what they want—"hoping" for things and "wishing" for events to happen.

I've heard "hope" referred to as "the language of the poor." Those who hope for things to work out, without taking steps towards working them out, are resigned to accept their position in this life, whatever it is.

Your goals should be written exactly as you want them. By *exactly,* I mean describing them as precisely and as specifically as is humanly possible, based on whatever characteristics your goal has that is important to you.

The purpose of being exact is so that you will know the precise instant that you have realized your goal. For example, let's say you want a new house within five years. Unless the type of house, location, size, and number of rooms, and all the other characteristics you have in mind are specified (including the ability to afford the house payments, taxes, and maintenance), you could end up owning a new house but experiencing grave disappointment in the specific home you've acquired.

A little trick that the mind pulls on us sometimes is to make it very reasonable to compromise a goal if it is not expressed exactly as we wanted it. For example, if you have a goal such as "I want a new house that is larger than this one, in a nice neighborhood," when you had in mind a four-bedroom, three-bath home in a very exclusive area of the country—you could end up achieving the goal as you expressed it, *but not as you wanted it!* In other words, you could have achieved owning a newer house, a bigger house in another neighborhood, and still not have completed the picture of the actual house you wanted. This could leave a lessened degree of satisfaction than you could have achieved had you expressed your goal clearly and *exactly.* Your mind might even make it into a "failure" of some kind.

When your goal is expressed exactly and specifically, there is no doubt at all when you have reached it and there is clear cause for celebration! I know some people who even draw pictures or "image" what they want, making the goal even more real for themselves. One man actually selected the house he wanted, picked the color he was going to paint it, and prepared a budget in order to decorate it exactly as he wanted it.

Remember, the more significant you plan to make your goal, the more exact you need to be about expressing it. Obviously, the need to be specific is minimized when the significance is reduced. To learn to ski for fun, for example, while still requiring some exactness about the level of expertise you want to achieve, need not be expressed as accurately and as succinctly as the same goal with a much higher significance—such as wanting to become an Olympic champion!

Set your goal so that there is no possible way that you could miss recognizing that you attained it. Be exact and precise and you will know.

WRITING GOALS

• *Write: Exactly When You Want It.* Goals need to have a deadline for their accomplishment.By definition, goals need to be specified within some kind of time framework. Goals cannot exist out of time. A goal is an event, a happening, an accomplishment, and, as such, requires a time zone for its attainment to be meaningful.

The largest time zone available to you, of course, is your lifetime. While your goals can be set for a nearly infinite number of deadlines, these deadlines will all be within your lifetime.

I recommend that deadlines for your goals be on an individual goal basis. Do not attempt to classify your goals with regard to one-year, two-year, or five-year deadlines. Let each goal or desire have its appropriate time for completion.

Deadlines for the accomplishment of your goals need to be exact—down to the exact day, in the case of short-term goals (the *time* of the day may even be an appropriate deadline, depending upon your particular goal). Remember that maximum satisfaction comes from accomplishment when it is manifested *exactly as* you wanted it, *exactly when* you wanted it.

• *Write: In Positive Language.* Goals written in a positive, affirmative manner tend to support accomplishment more than goals that are expressed as they relate to a negative or undesirable condition.

By writing the goal as a statement of the desired condition, and not as a function of changing the undesired condition, you do not need to drag around the old condition or situation you want to see behind you.

For instance, let's say you want to lose twenty pounds. Rather than writing your goal as a function of "losing" weight, a constant reminder of your *overweightness,* write your goal as a description of the way you want it—the new condition. If you weigh 160 pounds and you want to weigh 140 pounds, express your goal as "I weigh 140 pounds," not as "I have lost 20 pounds." State, "I am supportive of others," rather than, "I no longer criticize others." Carrying around the old, unwanted condition can be a burden and impair your progress.

This simple technique can save you considerable energy and, as a result, support the accomplishment of any of your goals with far less struggle and effort.

It is far easier to create a new, fresh condition than it is to alter, change, or remodel an older, established one. This approach has proven very valuable and I would like you always to keep this technique in mind when expressing your goals, here and in the future.

• *Write: As If It Exists Now.* The *present time* technique assists you in visualizing your goal as if it already exists. A goal stated in future time is likely to always remain in the future.

It has been found to be extremely valuable to state all goals as if they already existed. Like the positive, affirmative guideline, this does not burden you with the way things *used to be* or the way things *were* and avoids associating yourself with the struggle in that transformation.

Similarly, utilizing the present tense in your wants and desires assists you in picturing what you want as it will exist for you, not as something you want but do not have.

For example, instead of expressing a goal for having your teeth in perfect shape as, "I want my teeth and gums *to be* in perfect order by . . .," state, "It is [date] and my teeth and gums *are* in perfect order." Rather than writing, "I will . . .," write, "I am. . . ."

MAINTAIN YOUR LIST OF GOALS

Your goals list needs to be flexible and maintainable. Our lives in this physical universe are in a constant condition of change. Likewise, our desires, tastes, and personalities are in a constant state of fluctuation.

Since we live in an environment that represents change, our list of goals should be flexible, adjustable, and maintainable in order that we may continually review our list from a present-time position, appropriate to what our current situation is. It would make little sense, for instance, to be continually striving for a particular goal, simply because we stated it a year or two ago, regardless of whether or not we still want it. A goals list is not something that we write out once in our lifetime, etch it on stone, and bury it away for eternity. A goals list is a stated position of what we want for ourselves in our lives at any one particular given time.

In order to continue to expand the experience of satisfaction in our lives, we need to be continually in touch with our goals and monitor our progress towards their attainment. Quite often, when I'm reviewing my goals list, I notice that I have a lessening desire for an item that I had previously felt very strongly about. As a result, I will lower its priority, restate it, modify, or, sometimes, eliminate it totally from my goals list!

Later in this book, I'll discuss the benefits of tending to your goals in greater detail. I wanted to make the point here, however, that maintaining your goals list is extremely important for a continuing life of ongoing satisfaction.

Always have something ahead of you to look forward to, to work for . . . look forward, not backward.

Dr. Maxwell Maltz

CHAPTER VIII

PREPARING FOR THE ADVENTURE

We've covered some theory regarding goals. We've seen how resistant we humans can be when it comes to getting clearer about how we want our lives to be. I've given you the Focusing principle and some guidelines to keep in mind while listing what you want in your life.

It is now time to stop providing data—information designed to prepare you for listing your own personal goals. It is time to get on with the exercise itself. This listing process could be the most valuable experience of your life, depending upon how much previous attention you've given to your own well-being.

The purpose of this chapter is to give you all the instructions necessary to set up an environment in which you'll get maximum value from the experience of reviewing your current lifestyle and listing what you want.

Your surroundings should support you in this very exciting adventure and I'd like to offer you some suggestions so that you can be assured of this support.

The upcoming process can be extremely valuable for you, not only for its immediate benefit—new clarity and a clearer idea of how you want things to be—but also as a learning experience, which will allow you to repeat the exercise as often as you desire in the future.

You are about to embark on a journey that *can be* the most valuable trip you've ever *treated* yourself to. This adventure can be a fabulous, invigorating experience for you. The value you receive is a function of your willingness to look—to see how you want things to be.

SCHEDULE TIME

The next chapter consists solely of the Focusing exercise itself and I want you to plan on completing the entire exercise in one continuous block of time, allowing a minimum of four hours from the time you start the chapter to the time you complete the exercise. It is impossible to determine accurately how many hours each person might require, since the time period varies greatly for each individual. When I do one-to-one consultations or when I lead groups in this process, I have some control over the timing and scheduling of the exercises. In this format, however, you will have to judge for yourself and be responsible for keeping to your own schedule.

The amount of time you'll require will depend upon how many distractions you allow yourself, how much reverie you engage in, or any other detours you take. If you know that you tend to get distracted easily, if you are familiar with your attention span and the degree of difficulty you usually have in sticking to a project, you should allow an extra couple of hours.

Don't schedule something after the exercise that has a fixed time to happen. For example, don't have a dinner date or any other firm appointment. Don't have anything planned that *has* to happen at the conclusion of the alloted time for this exercise.

By having a planned appointment or event after your Focusing exercise, your mind will keep *some* attention on that appointment and distract you that much more. Also, you may start feeling a sense of urgency and feel rushed towards the conclusion of the exercise.

BE SURE TO HAVE ALL THE TIME YOU NEED TO COMPLETE THE PROCESS, WITHOUT FEELING RUSHED.

Keep your attention on the suggested topic and do not go off on nostalgic and sentimental excursions from the past. You can always do that later and, if you really want to do it, write it down on your list!

A time that would allow you to complete the exercise (without any consideration about having something to do after you are through) could be after an early dinner, starting the next chapter about 6:00 p.m., with nothing else planned for the entire evening except the exercise.

SELECT A PLACE

The physical environment you select will work best if it is free of distractions. Avoid any rooms or other surroundings that tend to distract you or cause your attention to stray. Very uninteresting rooms, with little or no decor items, plain walls and furniture, and otherwise unimposing atmospheres are helpful to maximize your concentration.

Make sure the place you select will be free of outside interruptions as well as having few distractions inside. If there is a telephone, disconnect it or isolate it so that you will never be aware of its ringing. Arrange it so that no one will intrude upon you and break your trend of thought. Be sure the children don't burst in on you. Are there any pets around? Will they be an intrusion?

Are there any other people who might drop in? Arrange for total isolation with your thoughts. I know that this may seem very odd and strange, but you need to be only with *yourself* if you are going to see what *you* want. You need *absolute privacy.* I recognize this will be a very strange experience for you—you've probably never done anything like this before, but do it anyway! Avoid having any views from windows that might be distracting. Radios and television sets are obvious items to exclude. No music or other sounds should be intruding on the atmosphere.

It usually works best to find a place that is totally *unfamiliar* to you, where there are no memories and no one knows of your presence.

Deborah, a 28-year-old housewife, rents an inexpensive motel room whenever she reviews her goals. The distractions are usually minimized due to the somewhat stark decor and no one else ever knows she is there. She leaves word at the manager's office to hold any telephone calls and she feels absolutely free of any outside interference while she looks at her life.

She feels that the $30 or $40 cost of the room is well worth the price in light of the value she receives from the experience. If you can afford it, I heartily suggest doing something similar. Get away from familiar terrain that holds memories and distractions.

Don't do the Focusing exercise with someone else! Several people have asked me if it would work to experience the process with someone very close to them, like their lover or spouse. Absolutely not! Again, this exercise is probably the first really *personal* thing you've every done for yourself. It is for *you alone!*

Doing it with a husband or wife may seem very romantic, but it would be disastrous as far as having any personal value to you. It could actually be damaging since you would be influenced heavily by the other person.

DO THE EXERCISE BY YOURSELF!

If you want to share your goals with someone afterward—great! I support that activity totally. I think that sharing goals contributes enormously to successful living and I'd like to see everyone communicate and promote what they want in life.

But, don't set your goals, don't plan your life—with anyone but yourself.

HAVE EVERYTHING WITH YOU

Make a very neat copy of the 8 guidelines as specified in Chapter VII. Headline these 8 guidelines on an 8½x11" sheet of paper to keep with you while doing the exercise.

Make sure that you have everything that you need when you sit down to begin the next chapter.

Be certain that your environment temperature will not cause a distraction. Have a sweater or coat available if you tend to get cold. Have good lighting—lighting to be writing by, since you will be doing a lot of listing on paper. If you are a cigarette smoker, check to see that you have plenty of cigarettes and matches. What about bathroom facilities?

Generally, make sure that you have everything that you need to eliminate any need to leave your selected area. Should you need to leave anyway, keep your attention on your goals. Minimize any other conversations with others and don't stay out of the room or away from your lists any longer than absolutely necessary.

Naturally, bring this book along with you and, perhaps, a clothespin, a large paperclip, or a spring-loaded clip—something to hold the pages of the book open while you are writing.

Have plenty of writing paper. I suggest an 8½x11" standard size tablet of lined notepaper, but select whatever you feel will work best for you. You'll be creating lists, perhaps *very extensive* lists. Keep this in mind when selecting your paper. I'd like to suggest that you use a fresh, *new* tablet, also. There is something special about starting with a brand new tablet.

A pen or pencil, whichever you prefer, is a rather obvious tool you'll be needing, but easy to forget. You might keep some spares handy to save the frustration of running out of ink or having a felt-tip pen dry up on you. If you are going to be using a pencil, make provisions for maintaining a sharp point.

Is there anything else you can think of? Knowing how you might act in this kind of situation and knowing that you need to concentrate on your goals throughout the Focusing exercise, is there anything else that you can do to prepare yourself for getting the most value from the exercise? If so, please do it. Write it down now and make sure that you do it before you begin the Focusing exercise—before you start the next chapter.

Summing up, then, before going any further in this book,

- schedule at least four continuous hours;
- select a quiet place, free of distractions; and
- have all the things you will need.

Once again I want to ask you to continue only after all of these things have been done—even if you have to wait several days. If you are about to devote four hours to looking at what you want, if you are on the brink of spending some very rare time to yourself, by yourself, if you are planning to take a giant step toward improving the quality of your life, then give it your best shot!

Don't cheat yourself by taking shortcuts. Don't ruin what otherwise might be an extremely valuable exercise. Begin the exercise with the intention to receive value from it. Continue through the exercise regardless of the temptations to wander.

Complete the exercise with the knowledge that you have truly looked for all the things that you wanted. Complete it with the knowledge that you aren't simply stopping because you are tired and time is running short.

Acknowledge that this will be a *very rare* experience for yourself. If you are like 99% of the people on this planet, this will be the first time you have ever spent *any* time looking at how you wanted your life to be, much less several hours. It's okay to celebrate the trip you are about to take. It takes some courage. *And,* remember my promise from Chapter VI.

Have you set a time to begin Chapter IX? Great!

The proper function of man is to live, not exist. I shall not waste my days trying to prolong them. I shall use my time.

Jack London

CHAPTER IX

THE FOCUSING EXERCISE

IMPORTANT: If more than a day has passed since you've read Chapter VIII, review it and verify that you are prepared to begin this chapter, including the commitment of time.

Since you have prepared yourself to complete this chapter in one single sitting, look around the immediate area in which you'll be spending the next several hours. Notice everything that interests you and become familiar with all the aspects, colors, textures, and shades of the physical environment—the walls, floor, ceiling, and furniture. If you are outdoors, notice the ground cover, the vegetation, the sky, and the horizon.

Remind yourself as to why you are here—why you are doing this exercise.

If you are a bit nervous, just acknowledge the feeling and let it be. Many people never allow themselves to get this far. Tim, an owner of an automobile service business, once explained to me that he felt that this life was quite comfortable and that he didn't want to "rock the boat." He refused to take the Focusing seminar. On the other hand, Bill, a printer and lithographer, acknowledged his nervousness about what he may have discovered, and attended the seminar anyway. Following the seminar, he informed me that he had found the experience to be extremely valuable, that he forgot all his misgivings soon after the Focusing exercise began.

You are going to be looking at everything you want in life. Since *everything* can seem extremely overwhelming and monumental, you will be looking at selected areas—one at a time.

There are three key areas at which you will be looking, one at a time:
- What you want for your experience of yourself.
- What you want regarding your interaction with others.
- What things you want from the physical universe.

As each goal or desire or dream comes to mind, write it down on your list, number it, and keep looking.

Don't feel that you need to have a goal just because a category is suggested. *All you want is to get your own true desires down on paper!* That's all. Don't manufacture any that don't exist! This is not an examination. Don't work your brain overtime to "figure out" any desires. We want "real" desires, not intellectual conceptualizations.

Make sure your goals are things you really want, not just some "good ideas." Do they "turn you on" or do they just sound good? How do they feel in your gut? Are they you or just the product of sound reasoning?

Will they feel good when you accomplish them or are they things you think your friends or parents would like to see you be, do, or have? Okay, are you ready?

WHAT I WANT FOR MY OWN EXPERIENCE OF MYSELF

Starting at the top of a clean sheet of paper, write: "What I want for my own experience of myself." Underline this headline and think about how you want to feel about yourself. Think about the kind of person you want to be.

Don't be concerned with objects, possessions, other people, relationships, or any other areas except you and things about yourself. You'll cover these other areas later.

Think about how you feel about yourself and all the criticisms, self-evaluations, judgments, and restraints you create for yourself.

Picture how you want to feel about yourself in the future.

Using the sheet of guidelines you copied out of Chapter VII, write down all the characteristics you want to have. If a date for their completion is associated with them—fine, write it down, too. However, don't force it. Just get down on paper what it is you want.

Now, regarding yourself, what do you really know that you want? What do you want for your own experience of yourself—of which you are *absolutely certain!*

What else do you know you want?

Regarding the kind of person you want to be, what do you want? Don't be concerned with how you are going to do it. Just get clear on what you want.

What do you want when it comes to you as a person, the way you want to be?

What is there about you, right now, that you are not pleased about? Write these things down. Start writing and complete the listing of that goal.

Keep looking for what you want regarding your own experience of yourself—that you are really clear and certain about.

Have you written down at least one goal?

Write! If you don't get anything, keep looking until you do. You surely have at least one other deisre for yourself—one aspect of your personality or character that you'd like to see changed, or improved, or different. What is it?

There you go—write it down now.

Keep looking for goals you are very sure about. Start them off by writing, "I am . . ." or "I am the kind of person . . ." or "I see myself as . . ." Picture yourself as being absolute perfection—the perfect man or woman. Now, see who that perfect person is; what characteristics of that perfection do you want?

What about knowledge or education? Are there things you want to know that you don't know now?

Are there projects, courses, classes, or other quests for added knowledge or education that you have started and want to finish?

In the area of formal education, do you have any goals regarding

- grammar school?

- high school?

- junior college?

- college?

- graduate school?

Are there any degrees or credentials you want to earn? Do you have any desires to take courses regarding your career, trade, or profession? Science or mathematics? Which ones? How about evening classes?

What desires, if any, do you have to improve physical abilities? In sports, do you want to take any lessons? Which ones:

- skiing?
- swimming?

- golf?
- horseback riding?

- tennis?
- sailing?

In regard to operating machinery, do you want to learn anything?

- driving a car?
- boats?

- flying an airplane?
- motorcycles?

- power tools?
- construction equipment?

- computer programming?
- typing?

In the area of hobbies, what do you want to learn? How about

- card games?
- chess?

- photography?
- art?

- sculpture?
- dancing?

- weaving?

Is there anything regarding education or knowledge that you want for improving your income?

- gaining financial worth?

- getting a promotion?

- advancing socially?

Regarding self-improvement, what do you want to learn?

- leadership?   - writing?

- assertiveness?   - languages?

- reading?   - consciousness?

- communication?   - effectiveness?

Do you want to learn anything that is a practical skill around the house?

Are there any correspondence classes you want to take?

- what else do you want to learn?

What do you want regarding your own personal development? What courses could you take to learn what you want to know?

- what don't you know now, that you'd like to know?

Is there anything else you'd like regarding education or gaining additional knowledge about anything?

Get them all written down.

If you can't think of any more, but you feel or sense that there are more to come, leave some extra lines. You can come back later and add more when you think of them. Make a note in the margins to remind you where you left off.

What about health?

Regarding your body, what do you want? What do you want for your body that doesn't exist now? How about

- diet?
- muscle tone?

- physical condition?
- exercise?

What parts of your body need attention?

- heart
- eyes

- lungs
- hair

- ears
- stomach

- feet
- throat

- sinus
- spine

What have you been procrastinating about?

- What about your teeth?

- What medical people do you want to see?

What physical condition have you been putting up with? Is there something you want to do about it? What is it?

What recreation, rest, relaxation, or stress-reducing activities do you sincerely want to start doing?

Habits to stop:

● drinking?   ● smoking?

● overeating?   ● other? _____

What shape and measurements do you want to be? Remember, write them down as you want them, in the present tense, as affirmations.

What aren't you doing for your physical well-being that you really want to begin doing for it?

Is there anything else regarding health that you'd like to start doing, investigate or look into, stop doing, do more of, do less of, pay more attention to, or otherwise alter?

Write them down.

Leave some extra space in case you think of anything else.

What about your attitude towards yourself? Do you want to alter any attitudes you have about your own

- temperament?
- fears and emotions?

- habits and patterns?
- likeability?

- confidence/ decision-making?
- guilts/anxieties?

- upsets/problems?
- independence?

How about your

- energy and ambition?
- talent and abilities?

- drive and affinity?
- nervousness?

- level of responsibility?
- morals and standards?

Do you want to change your experience of yourself as

- an intelligent person?
- a knowledgeable person?

- a strong person?
- being okay?

- a deserving person?
- being capable?

- being ethical?
- being powerful?

- an attractive person?
- being responsible?

- being successful?
- a good person?

- being artistic?

About now, you might be feeling like you are really getting into some old murky stuff—like walking through a swamp. Upon reaching this point, a professional writer had the feeling that he was "in a musty attic, full of clutter that has been ignored for years and years."

What kind of self-evaluation do you do on yourself regularly? What personal faults do you keep coming up with? What positive qualities do you want? What negative qualities do you want to rid yourself of? How can you stop attacking your own self-esteem?

Do you want to alter your attitude about yourself as

- a selfish person?
- a creative person?

- a sexual person?
- being satisfied?

- a self-disciplined person?
- a happy person?

- being sensitive?
- being talented?

- being romantic?
- a jealous person?

- being spiritual?
- a fun person?

- being sociable?
- a lazy person?

Do you want to feel

- more graceful and coordinated?
- more understanding?

- more aware or curious?
- more adventurous?

- more personable?
- more supportive of others?

What attitudes do you hold about yourself now that you'd like to get rid of?

How do you want to feel about yourself that you are not feeling now?

Is there anything else you want to do about your personal attitude about yourself—your own self-esteem?

What about the way you live?

Is there anything about your lifestyle, your daily routine, your feelings about every-day living that you want to change, alter, or eliminate?

What do you want for yourself that would be delightful—a joy? What treats could you provide yourself? What extravagances would you like for your own personal satisfaction—not anyone else's—just yours?

How about time? Do you have any goals with respect to having more time or less time? What about being late, or on time, for appointments? What about efficiency and using time effectively?

Do you feel pressured a lot of the time? Do you want to do something about it? What do you want to do?

Do you have any incomplete projects that you want to complete? What are they? Write them down.

Do you have any incomplete projects that you don't want to finish? Will it be okay for you to complete them mentally and drop them from your mind? If so, which ones are they?

Is there anything about your daily routine that you want to change? Do you have any goals with respect to daily happenings that affect the quality of your life? If so, what are they? With regard to your daily life, do you have any goals affecting the place where you live? Where you work? Where you play?

What specific, exact goals do you have about how you experience daily living in terms of quality? Do you want to increase the quality of your daily life? Do you want to demand more perfection in your life?

What things aren't okay the way they are? What do you want to do about it?

What goals do you have about the way you transport yourself, how you get around on a daily basis?

Don't be concerned if you aren't getting any insights on *all* these categories; they are designed to trigger goals you *may* have in that particular area. If you don't have any, if nothing registers, don't force it and invent anything—just keep looking.

Do you have any goals regarding your purpose in life? Do you realize your own purpose? Do you want to realize it?

Do you have any other goals for your every-day style of life? Write them down.

Remember, be exact, and list your goals as if they already existed and the way you want them to be; don't keep dragging the current unwanted condition around with you.

How about self-expression? Do you feel you are currently expressing yourself as fully as you want to?

In terms of communication,

- do you feel effective?

- do you feel open?

- do you feel you accomplish what you want to?

- how about writing and composition?

- what about speaking ability?

- do you want to write to people more often?

- what things do you want?

- what abilities do you want?

What do you do now that you want to stop doing? Do you want to call people more frequently? What things do you want to say that you aren't saying?

With regard to expressing your creativity, what do you want regarding

- art?   - carving?

- sculpture?   - painting?

- watercolor?   - photography?

- mosaic?   - design?

- writing?   - clothing?

Do you have any goals with respect to

- acting on stage?

- writing poetry?

- writing a book?

- playing a musical instrument?

- singing or any other performing?

Have you discovered any new desires and wants within yourself? What are they? Write them down.

Self-expression goals are frequently buried deeper than other hidden desires. Do not suppress your desire to express yourself. Take whatever desires come up for you and write everything down. You can always look it over later and sharpen it in detail, but get it on your list for now. If you aren't sure, write it down anyway. After all, what does it cost you?

Do you have any other wants regarding these areas:

- personal enhancement?   • lifestyle?

- self-improvement?   • self-expression?

- creativity?   • health?

- learning?   • attitude?

- education?   • self-esteem?

What are they? Have you written them down? Get your thoughts on paper. You can always come back and revise the working of your goals to conform to our guidelines.

Regarding the kind of person you want to be, do you have any other desires for yourself? Are there any other things you want to add to your experience of yourself—in the near future or further out in future?

Write them down.

Picture yourself as being absolutely perfect—EXACTLY the way you want to be. Okay? Are all the things that need to happen for you to be perfect on your list? If all the goals you just listed were realized, would you be perfect? If not, what else needs to happen? What else do you want?

Imagine that all the goals you've listed have come true for you. Now say, "I am absolutely perfect!" Does that feel real for you? If not, why? See what else needs to happen for you to feel perfect. Write it down.

WHAT I WANT REGARDING MY INTERACTIONS WITH OTHERS

Starting on a new sheet of paper, write the following heading at the top of the page: "What I want regarding my interaction with others." Underline the heading.

In the area of doing something for some other person or group, what do you want to do? What contributions do you want to make to your

- immediate family?

- other family members?

  - brothers/sisters?

  - grandparents?

  - mother/father?

  - cousins?

  - wife/husband?

  - aunt/uncles?

  - son/daughter?

  - grandchildren?

- other loved ones?

  - stepparents/stepchildren?

  - half-brothers/sisters?

  - other relatives?

If you have an ex-husband or ex-wife, is there anything you want to do for him or her?

Don't be thinking about what you can do for someone to gain advantage or have them owe you. Just look for those things you may want to do for someone just because you want to.

If you are living with someone, is there a specific contribution you want to make to his or her life?

Is there something you really want to do for

- old friends?
- girlfriends?
- boyfriends?
- school chums?
- friends from work?
- new friends?
- old lovers?
- new lovers?
- roommates?
- anyone else?

Is there any neighbor you want to do something for?

If you are in business, what about

- partners?
- your employer?
- supervisors?
- subordinates?
- co-workers?

If you are a student, what about your teachers, fellow students, or school administrators?

With regard to groups and organizations, do you want to do anything for

- any fraternal organization?
- your social club?
- your church?
- classes you are in?
- civic groups?

- political parties?
- movements or causes?
- neighborhood associations?
- sporting clubs?
- any other group?

In the governmental area, do you really want to contribute to

- your city?
- your county?

- your state?
- your country?

Regarding mankind, what do you want to do for

- the planet?
- science?

- the universe?
- ecology?

Do you have a desire to solve universal problems such as

- disease?
- pollution?
- overpopulation?
- hunger and starvation?

- political oppression?
- military conflict?
- any other areas?

Is there something that you'd really like to do for a close friend? A confidant? A coffee pal? Someone other than anyone else you've thought of so far?

Do you have a desire to run for election

- as a politician?
- as a union official?
- as a school class officer?
- within your club?

- in your trade association?
- in the PTA?
- any other group or club?

Is there any other deed, contribution, or action you want to take on behalf of any person or group?

Write it down. Write exactly what you really want to do.

In the area of communication, what do you want to be, do, or have that you are not being, doing, or having now?

Do you want to improve your

- willingness to speak to others?
- openness and frankness?
- ability to deliver your message?
- concentration?
- ability to listen to others?

Is there a specific problem you experience frequently while communicating that you want to work on? What is it? Write it down.

Do any of the following questions suggest a goal for you?

- Are you bashful?

- Do you withhold part of yourself?

- Do you mix with people easily?

- Are you gregarious?

- Do you say everything you want to?

- Are you frequently lonely?

- Do you exclude yourself?

I'm not suggesting that these are true for you, but you may want to work on one of more of these areas.

Do you want to express yourself more fully regarding

- love and affection?

- hate or anger?

- disapproval/disagreement?

- saying yes?

- saying no?

Regarding entertaining and social situations, do you have any specific goals about

- dating?
- being in groups/crowds?

- having parties?
- feeling part of the group?

- going to parties?

What do you want people to know that you aren't telling them? What part of yourself are you holding back? Do you want to change these patterns? Write down what you want to do.

Is there anything else, regarding your communications with others, that you want and don't have?

Is there something about your communications that you don't have now, but you really want?

Regarding your relationships with others, how do you want them to be? What do you want to have in your relationships that you don't have now?

Specifically, how do you want your relationship to be with your family?

- your husband or wife?
- your parents?

- your children?
- other members of your immediate family?

- your brothers or sisters?

How do you want to relate to those people you live with?

- husband or wife?   • children?

- roommates?   • others?

- lover?

What do you really want out of your relationships at work?

- with your fellow workers?

- with your boss?

- with your subordinates?

- with business associates?

What type of romantic relationship do you want? Describe it in detail. Specify what you want in that "perfect" relationship. What is the first step you can take toward realizing a relationship like this? Write down what you want in the relationship AND what you can do to make it happen.

What old disagreements could be improved?

- parents?   • people who reared you?

- ex-spouses?   • children who left?

- former lovers,   • people with whom you
  boyfriends, girlfriends?   had a disagreement?

111

Look carefully and see if you have any unresolved relationships with a pet, perhaps a dog or a cat. Are you carrying around any guilt feelings with regard to a pet you had once? Or still have? What can you do to clear it up now?

Do you have any specific objectives regarding your relationship with God? Or your innerself? Or the supreme being in you? Or Christ? Or the Self? The Tao? Or whatever you call the natural order of things?

Would you like to resolve anything or clear any relationship with anyone who is no longer living? Yes, you can do something about your relationships with people who have died. If you want to, just demonstrate your willingness to do it and write it down.

What relationships do you have that you don't want?

What relationships do you want that you don't have?

Write them down in detail.

Regarding the way others experience you, what do you want?

WRITE:

• **"Other people experience me as _____."** (Complete the sentence for yourself. If you have several goals for this, write them all down, one at a time.)

Regarding your appearance, how do you want others to observe you?

- wardrobe?

  - clothes?
  - shoes?

  - style?
  - condition?

- hairstyle?

  - length?
  - color?

  - style?
  - condition?

- complexion?

  - tan?
  - makeup?

  - condition?
  - healthy?

- aliveness?

  - glow?
  - energy level?

  - smile or frown?

What else do you want others to see in you?

What mannerisms do you have that don't support you? What mannerisms do you have that you don't want? What mannerisms do you want that you don't have now?

Are there any habits that you want to eliminate? Do any of the following suggestions stimulate you? If so, write down the ones that are really significant for you, personally:

- interrupting people when they are talking?
- talking loudly?

- bragging?
- talking softly?

- judging others?
- not talking at all?

- impressing people?
- borrowing things?

- driving too fast?
- being righteous?

- not participating?
- holding back?

- being late?
- not keeping agreements?

- being sloppy?

With respect to your attitude towards others, what do you want? (Look at prejudices, bias, arrogance, superiority, inferiority, fear of others, defensiveness, dominating, being dominated, blaming others, accepting blame, and withdrawing from others.)

In the area of sex, what do you want that you don't have? What is going on now that you want to be different? Write down the way you want things.

Are there any other wants and desires, any other goals, that you have for what you want regarding how you interact and relate with other people?

WHAT THINGS I WANT FROM
THE PHYSICAL UNIVERSE

Starting once again with a new sheet of paper, headline this page, "What things I want from the physical universe." Underline the heading.

Now we are going to look at physical possessions, objects, earthly wealth—the "stuff" part of life. We'll look at what you want to do—activities, vocations, careers, and what you want from them. Whatever you want from the organizations, the government, society, the planet—anything you want from the physical universe for yourself.

Starting this area with your career or vocation, what do you want that you don't have currently?

If you were working in the perfect business, one that you would describe as being perfect for you, what would it be? What do you want out of it?

- recognition?
- acknowledgement?

- challenge?
- financial reward?

What do you want in your career that you don't have?

- advancement?
- satisfaction?

- status?
- contentment?

- future?

What ambitions do you have for your career? Do you want

- to work for a large company?

- to work for a small company?

- to work for yourself?

If you don't have a job working for an employer or for yourself, what do you consider your job in life to be? Mother? Housewife? Someone who just hangs out? Well, then, just what do you want out of whatever you do—whatever you consider your "job" to be.

Regarding progress and advancement, do you want to be promoted? To what position? By whom? Do you need to take courses to advance? What incentives do you have to advance?

Picture yourself in the perfect job or business. Look and see if it really excites you. See if it "turns you on." If so, what do you need to do to begin realizing progress towards this goal?

First, write it down.

Regarding your experience of having enough time, what do you want that you don't have now? Do you have too much time? Do you want more things to do? Do you want more free time? Do you want fewer things to do?

Regarding efficiency, what would you like:

● manage your time better?   ● be more effective?

● plan your days better?   ● what else?

● take on fewer projects?

If you had free time, what would you like to do?

• vacation?

  • where?   • how?

  • how long?

• play sports?

  • which ones?   • how often?

• start new projects?

  • which projects?   • what hobbies?

  • take up new hobbies?   • nothing at all?

• travel?

  • by boat?   • by car?

  • by plane?   • where?

• what else?

Come on, you know how you've always wanted to do those things "if only you had the time"—let's go! What things? Write them down.

Describe your goals in great detail—in writing. Is there anything else you'd like to have regarding time?

Concerning money, what are your goals? Do you really want money? If so, in what form, or in what context do you want it? What does "having money" mean to you? Is it income or an amount stashed away?

- Do you have specific goals regarding your earnings?

- Specify how you want it:

    - weekly?

    - monthly?

    - annual salary?

- How about your savings account?

- Your checking account?

- Your safe deposit box?

- Your net worth?

What ideas do you have about money that you don't want to have? Do you have some preconceived ideas about money that create problems for you in getting it, keeping it, or having it? What ideas do you want to have about money? How would you like to think of money so that you could earn it with less struggle?

Don't worry or wonder how you can change your ideas about money; just decide whether or not you really want to change them.

In the areas of loans, financing, and debt, what do you want regarding:

- paying off your loans?

- collecting money owed to you?

- taking out a new loan?

- paying certain bills?

- settling disputes about money?

Do you sense that you have any barriers to having money? If so, do you really want to overcome them? If you do, describe them and state your goal as a positive activity toward overcoming those barriers.

Are there any specific kinds of investments that you particularly want? Do you care what form your investments are in?

If you want a specific type of investment, is it:

- shares of stock?

- being a partner in a business?
- bonds or notes?

- gas, oil, or minerals?

- gems or jewelry?

- options?

- real estate?

- residential?

- commercial?

- industrial?

- income producing?

- unimproved land?

- farms?

- some other form?

What profits do you want your investments to make to you? Specify your goals for profit in terms that leave no question—percentage of annual return, cash flow, appreciation, shelter, etc.

You don't need to know all this terminology; if you want to make money from investing, make your goal to start an investment plan and select someone to counsel you in doing it.

Regarding physical objects, or tangible property, what do you want? Describe your desires in explicit detail.

Do you have a specific goal regarding a home?

- What type?

    - house?
    - condominium?
    - apartment?
    - co-op?

- Where?

    - city?
    - country?
    - suburbs?
    - neighborhood?
    - location?
    - weather?

- What size?

    - square footage?
    - number of bedrooms and baths?

- What amenities do you want?

  - pool?   - sauna?

  - landscaping?   - showers?

  - sprinklers?   - carpets?

  - fireplaces?

- What architectural design do you want?

  - ranch-style?

  - colonial?

  - townhouse?

- What price?

Do you want a second home, now or in the future?

- What type?

- Where?

- What amenities?

- What size?

Are there any other forms of homes, residences, or places to stay that you want to own, lease, or otherwise possess for your own use?

How about vehicles?

- Automobiles:

  - make?
  - model?
  - color?

  - year?
  - accessories?
  - new or used?

- How about boats?

  - what size?

  - for fishing, skiing, pleasure?

Or how about:

- a plane?
- motorcycle?
- camper?
- motorhome, van, pickup truck?

- 4-wheel drive, jeep, snowmobile?
- tractor?
- race car?

For your own hobby uses, do you have any goals to own items, gear, tackle, or equipment related to

- fishing?
- boating?
- hunting?
- camping?
- hiking?

- cooking?
- rafting?
- gliding?
- skiing?
- other?

How about tools? Are there any power tools or hand tools you want to have that you don't have now?

How about sporting goods of any other kind?

Still regarding hobbies, are there any clubs or organizations you want to join?

Do you have any other goals for

- things you wear?
- things you work with?
- things with motors?
- things you have fun with?

With respect to furnishings, things around and inside your home (either the one you have now or the one you want), what specific desires do you have regarding

- furniture?
- appliances?
- antiques?
- bedrooms?
- living room?
- kitchen?
- den?
- dining room?
- musical equipment?
- floors?
- landscaping?
- keepsakes?
- decorating?

- carpet?
- draperies?
- paintings?
- cabinets?
- garage?
- lighting?
- plants?
- china?
- silverware?
- linen?
- modernizing?
- other improvements, additions, or changes?

If you have an office, are there things you want regarding furnishings such as:

- furniture?
- carpet?
- draperies?
- wall hangings?

- plants?
- office equipment?
- desk accessories?
- cabinets?

In the area where you spend most of your time (your office, your home, at your desk, in your car), what changes do you want to make?

What true desires do you have regarding clothes or wardrobe?

- for formal wear?
- daily wardrobe?
- casual dress?
- sports attire?
- footwear?

- shoes, boots, sandals?
- hats?
- coats?
- jewelry, furs, purses, accessories?

What kind of feeling do you want when you open up your closet to select clothes to wear? Set your goals for acquiring those things that will provide you with that feeling.

Will your goals for your wardrobe support your goals for how you want to be observed and experienced by others? When wearing the clothes you want, will you feel the way you want to feel? Will it get you the desired result?

What physical sensations do you want to experience for yourself? What tastes and aromas do you want in your future? What sights do you want to see? What sounds do you want to hear? What about the future, near and far? What do you want to feel? Are there foods you want to taste, wines or other liquids to sip or sample? Are there surfaces you want to feel? Textures? What about music? What sounds do you want to hear?

What do you want to fix? What do you own or use that needs fixing in order for you to be getting maximum value from owning or using it?

How about the car?

- Is it free of dents?

- How is the paint?

- What about the way it runs?

- Is the transmission okay?

- Does it need tires?

What will it take to get the car into a condition that will free you of any concerns about whether or not it will work for you? Are you willing to get it fixed so that it can improve the quality of your existence?

How about where you live? Does everything work the way it should? Do all the appliances work? How about the plumbing? Does the place where you live need paint? Do the walls or floors need work? What maintenance needs to be done? What do you need to give some attention to? What have you been putting off— something that you've been avoiding? Do you want the things you've surrounded yourself with to work?

Do you have any specific desires to take long trips that you have not yet listed? What kind of trip do you want to take?

- Alone?

- With someone else?

- Who?

- International?

  - Europe?
  - Asia?
  - Africa?

  - Canada?
  - South America?
  - Australia?

How do you want to take your trip?

- by plane?
- by tour ship?
- by luxury liner?

- by sailboat?
- by automobile?
- first class or tourist?

Where do you want to stop and stay over? How long do you want to take?

What do you want to see in your own country? How do you want to travel domestically?

What other trips do you want to take? When? For how long?

List all the places you really truly want to see some day and allow them to become a real goal for you, not just a pipe dream. Take the first step in making your dreams and fantasies become real!

OKAY, TAKE A ONE-MINUTE BREAK.

Save your place in this book and stand up and move around for about one minute. Stretch out any tightened muscles and work out any knots you may have developed in your anatomy.

Congratulate yourself for having taken a very significant step toward getting your life in order—the way you want it to be EXACTLY. We're not through yet, but it is okay to take this opportunity to pat yourself on the back and revel in your accomplishment to this stage.

OKAY, THE BREAK IS OVER. SETTLE DOWN AGAIN AND HERE WE GO!

ALL SOULS FREE

Now that you've taken some time to acknowledge yourself for having created a comprehensive-appearing list of things you want in your life, let us do some more looking. Let's look at what your intentions are in life, regardless of some of the barriers you may have to expressing these intentions.

Look at what you've written down and notice what intentions, wants, or other real desires you may not have included.

Quite often, at this point, people will find themselves at a new level of awareness of their *true* intentions. Stay open and willing to look at whether or not you've written down all your goals. It is quite possible that your really true desires—your real intentions for your life—may be ready to surface, if they have not already done so. Don't keep them subdued if they want to surface.

Maintain your integrity. Stay true to what your real intentions are.

You cannot keep your integrity and walk through life with manufactured "wants" or "goals." Your intentions for your life, your real desires and wants, are what you want to have a clear picture of. If you have been subduing them for years and creating a lot of flak and cover to camouflage them, you may find the unveiling process a little uncomfortable. If so, acknowledge this discomfort and keep going—to the "real" goals you have, a precise alignment with your own true intentions.

There still may be some deeply buried desires within you. Sometimes these may be the biggest and most significant ones, too!

So, let's see what else we can find, okay?

With your lists in front of you, think about what you would really like to be that you were *too ashamed* to write down. What dream, what deep-seated desire have you been holding onto about the kind of person you are that you've kept a secret because you were ashamed to acknowledge it?

Write it down.

What things do you want to do that you've been too ashamed to list? What activity would you like to engage in that you've held back because you feel ashamed? What events would you like to see take place, so long as you didn't have to be concerned with other people's evaluation?

Write it down!

What is that item that you've always had a secret desire for—or that place you've often fantasized about? What else have you felt ashamed about wanting? Do you really want it? What is your intention about that item?

Picture yourself without shame.

Picture yourself as being incapable of feeling ashamed.

Now, what desires do you have, what is your intention in life? Do you still need to feel ashamed about wanting that thing or those things? Is it still appropriate to be concerned with that self-imposed judgment of yourself?

Has *embarrassment* prevented you from expressing your intentions, desires, or real wants? Look at your lists and see what you don't have listed because you'd be embarrassed for anyone to know about it.

What would you really like to do if you were not concerned about embarrassment? What activities would you like to engage in? What games would you like to play? What level of participation would you like to achieve if you didn't think about being embarrassed?

Has embarrassment been a barrier or a block for you in recognizing any desires? Has it been a source of conflict for you in getting everything you want out of life?

Picture yourself as being incapable of embarrassment. When you have that picture, really choose what you want to do, what you want to have, the kind of person you want to be.

What things would you like to have if you wouldn't feel so embarrassed about having them?

What things would you really like to do if you wouldn't feel so embarrassed in doing them?

At this time, look and see if you have your guard up. See if you are reacting defensively.

Are you resisting this new look at what you might really want? Are you being cool? Are you just glancing at these words—not really participating?

Let me warn you—this is where most people's subdued desires come to the surface. You could have some real "biggies" buried—things you've been denying yourself for years!

It's all up to you, so keep looking.

If you were absolutely guaranteed that no one else would ever see your list, and you were firmly convinced that this was so, what would you list as a goal, as an accurate statement of your intentions, that you have not yet written down?
Add it to your list.
Is there anything you want to be that you felt was *too silly* to include on your list? Whatever it is that suggested that giggle is what we're looking for.
Write it down.
Remember, no one is going to see your list unless you show it to them.
Now—what things do you want to do or have that would be too silly to write down?
If you think you might want something and you aren't quite sure, write it down anyway. You can always scratch it off later. Get it down in writing now, before the mousetrap closes on you.
Anything else?
Write all the silly desires, all the silly wants, all the silly fantasies down on your list. Are these statements of what you intend to see happen in your life?
Now, write down anything that you may want, but you think it's *too crazy.* You know, if *they* knew you wanted that, *they'd* probably lock you up. Yes, all those little goodies. Write them down.
What crazy things would you like to do or have that you haven't written down yet?

What have you thought of and then discounted because you figured that that was just your ego talking? What desires have you had come up that you've invalidated for any other reason?
Write those down, too!
What have you desired or wanted that you are just *unwilling to write down?* Fine—now write it down anyway!

- What are you *afraid* to want?

- What do you think you want, but it sounds too ordinary? Write it down.

- What do you think you want, but it *isn't significant enough?* Write it down.

- Is there anything else going on in your head? *Write it down,* whether you're sure or not!

- Write it *all* down.

- Don't move on until you have completed all of this.

TAKE A WALK

Close your eyes and envision yourself going through your home, room by room. Picture yourself investigating every nook and cranny of wherever you live and look at what you want to be, do, or have with respect to anything that comes up!
Use your home environment to trigger any other goals you may have. Once you have this idea clearly in your mind, close your eyes and mentally go all through the house, or apartment, and check it out thoroughly.
Write down anything you get, AS SOON AS YOU GET IT!
Now, do the same exercise with your office, or where you work, where you play, or wherever you spend time.
Write down whatever you get!
Mentally, go through desk drawers, the closets, the lockers, cupboards, boxes, and all those other hiding places.

Now, go through all the other places where you spend time. Go through your car — the glove compartment, the trunk, everywhere. Mentally check over the exterior of your car.

Is there anything else you *want to do* or *want to have* about these places that you haven't written down?

Is there anything you want to complete, alter, repair, remodel, return, loan or borrow, or paint?

- What actions do you want to take?
  Write them down.

- What attitudes do you want to adopt?
  Write them down.

What chores, agreements, or projects do you want to complete in order to have all these physical spaces and environments work for you totally and supportively?

IS THAT REALLY ALL?

So, now, are there any more items inside of you—any other desires or goals that you haven't written down that you are holding back? Are all of your intentions documented on your lists?

What if you were given the news that you had terminal cancer and that you had six months to live? You will be leaving this world in a half year!

Do you have any more goals in there? Aha, you might have found another one, you say? Great! Write it down.

What if you had one month's notice that our planet would collide with another terrestrial body and the world would cease to exist in its current form? What personal goals would you want to see realized then?

Okay, write it down.

Is there anything you would want to communicate? Experience? Hear? See? Taste?

Write them down.

No more looking? If you are totally empty and feel void of any additional desires:

TAKE A FULL MINUTE—SIXTY SECONDS.
BREATHE DEEPLY—INHALE . . . EXHALE—FOR A
FULL MINUTE.
DO NOTHING ELSE . . .

See if any more comes up. Write down any goals that come up.
Is that it? For sure?
Relax and take a break.
Give yourself permission to celebrate completing the exercise. Acknowledge yourself for having completed it, for having had the courage to begin it, and the willingness to continue.

I never think of the future. It comes soon enough.

Albert Einstein

CHAPTER X

SETTING DEADLINES

In order for a goal to be *completely* expressed, it needs to include a specific time frame in which it is to be accomplished, achieved, or attained, reflecting the intention of the person who sets the goal. For instance, while our own lifetime represents a maximum time limit, the time period for one particular football game may represent the maximum time framework in which a Super Bowl quarterback may be able to realize one of his lifetime goals—to win a Super Bowl!

Many goals have inherent time deadlines within themselves, time deadlines that cannot be separated from the results wanted, such as, "winning the 1988 Olympic Gold Medal." There are only a few days in the year of 1988 in which this goal can be accomplished—at the Games themselves.

A goal for having two thousand dollars in a savings account is far different if it is to be accumulated over a five-year period than if it were deadlined for a period of 18 months in the future.

EXACT DATES

Dates for accomplishing specific goals should be as *exact* as the goals themselves.

Quite often, in a goal-setting session, someone would tell me that they wanted to retire by a certain age without setting a specific date. For example, they'd say, "I want to retire by the time I'm forty." This statement gives them a full year in which to accomplish retirement (the year during which they are forty years old) where as they may have really wanted to be retired by their fortieth birthday (by the date itself)! Express yourself clearly as to what you really want, whether it is *by* your fortieth birthday or *before* your forty-first birthday, and use a date as your deadline.

REVIEW YOUR LISTS

Review your lists and set a date by which you want each goal to occur. Take plenty of time for this and be careful not to get too many things due on the same dates. Don't get more than you can handle. Each of us has our own idea of what is too much for us, so state your deadlines consistent with your own assessment of your abilities and energies.

By doing this exercise, *you are planning your life.* It could all change in the near future and adjustments are surely going to be in order, but, right *now,* you are working with all the things you want in your life and planning on when you want them all to happen. The nature of your goals may include a built-in date for final realization. For instance, the scheduling of an event you want to attend, the sequence in which related goals are achieved, and other criteria may have already determined deadline dates for some of your goals.

As a personal example, I have a specific goal relating to the celebrating of an anniversary. No matter how ambitious I am, I cannot move up the date of this anniversary. It happens when it happens. So my goal has an automatic deadline date, which corresponds to the anniversary date.

Other personal goals, which do not depend or relate to other circumstances, rely only upon your desire and intention for deadlines. You assign them a date, based on your own pace. It is just like planning a vacation trip, a tour, or a college curriculum.

Take your time. Be complete.

Make sure every stated goal has its own date for completion. No generalities or ambiguities. Only specific dates for each one to happen.

SUBGOALS

Goals will sometimes generate "subgoals" (or things that need to be done in order to achieve the main goal). These subgoals frequently resemble activities or "things do to" lists. When this kind of "to do" list is generated in order to accomplish a given goal, don't confuse the "subgoal" with the real objective or your intention. I've seen people confuse subgoals with their intentions and I've done it myself. Writing down your goals tends to keep you clear on the end result you want and it can save you wasting energy on accomplishing tasks or "subgoals" that don't lead to the desired final result.

For example, Mary wanted to obtain a real estate broker's license and certain college level courses were required, among other prerequisites. Mary planned out all the necessary things that needed to happen in order to get her broker's license. In taking one of her required courses, Mary felt frustrated due to a final grade she received. She passed the course without any problem, but her grade was less than she felt she should have earned.

When she looked at the entire scope of this adventure, Mary realized that she was right on her target path towards getting her license, well within the time she had allocated for it. However, she had made the taking of this one course (a task she needed to perform to reach her goal) just as significant as if it was her main goal!

The truth was that she had no desire to take the course EXCEPT to satisfy the requirements to attain her goal. The course was simply something that needed doing along the way. Mary had made her task or "subgoal" into a main goal in her mind, and, as a result, felt as though she had not performed satisfactorily.

You need to retain your own perspective on what ultimate result you want. Don't confuse the activities with the end result, however.

HOW DO YOU FEEL?

Right now, with your list in front of you, how do you feel about what you've created? Are you feeling excited and enthused?

Are you feeling invigorated and anxious to move on?

Have you discovered some valuable things about yourself?

Do you have a new awareness of how you tend to run your life?

Have you realized any unexpected results?

If you are feeling positive and ready to move on, then do so. Continue on to the next chapter and do not read any further in this chapter.

If you are feeling confused and overwhelmed by your list (because it's too long, too vague, too sloppy, too contradictory, or whatever), don't decide that you've messed it up! You are where most people seem to end up after listing all the things they want in their lives.

This phenomenon you are experiencing is related to your having confronted all those things you've ignored for so long—all the denial, procrastination, non-deservingness, fear, and doubt.

If you feel as though your list is too long or too confusing, that it will somehow get in your way to continuing and receiving value, then let us pause for a moment and look at the situation.

Look at your list and see what you could do so that you could continue and feel good about continuing. What could you add, take away, or alter on your list so that you could proceed and get value? If it feels too sloppy, could you rewrite it more neatly? Do you need to weed out some contradictory goals?

What attitude about your list and the process itself can you adopt, reject, or change that would let you continue and receive value?

Look and see what you can do, how you can be, or what attitude you can have to go on from here, being responsible about your own integrity.

Once you are ready to continue, proceed to the next chapter.

In the long run, we shape our lives, and we shape ourselves. The process never ends until we die. And the choices we make are ultimately our own responsibility.

Eleanor Roosevelt

CHAPTER XI

TENDING YOUR INTENTIONS

Now that you've created this list of what you really want and when you want it, you have started some movement in your life. The process that you've just completed has overcome the inertia of standing still. Now that you have invested the energy to start your life moving, you will require much less energy to keep it moving, to maintain the momentum.

I like the analogy of the rocket launching, where approximately one-half of all the fuel for a NASA launch is burned in raising the rocket that very first foot off the launching pad! Since more energy is required to start mass moving than is required to keep it in motion, you can see that most of your energy has been expended in getting this far. Now, all you have to do is to keep your life moving.

You have left the launching pad; you are on your way to the moon! Now, all you need to do is monitor your progress, correcting as necessary, and *keep* planning your life.

If you let it all settle back onto the launch pad, wasting all the energy that was used to get where you are, you will just have to go through it all over again sometime later, if you want to start getting what you want in life.

You have now created momentum. You have begun the ascent to having a more fulfilling and satisfying life. How do you keep it moving? By staying on top of how you are doing; by monitoring your progress towards your goals; by tending to your intentions and making sure that your integrity is kept intact—that you truly intend all these things to manifest themselves in your life; by checking what your *intentions* are and comparing them with your performance.

PLANNING

A goals list can look rather ominous to many people, representing a sometimes overwhelming and seemingly impossible list of things they want. I strongly feel that this is the place where most people will say to themselves, "Geez, I *thought* this was going to be hopeless, and now I *know* it is."

Despair tends to creep in here sometimes, when our minds are convinced that we have bitten off more than we can chew. This phenomenon is just more of all that junk we highlighted earlier—all the considerations and concepts that we bought in our earlier years. Ignore it, press on, and continue toward what you clearly want.

Once your goals are listed, along with your time deadlines, it is a rather simple process of going through them one by one and listing the activities that need to be done in order to attain your goals. This is called "planning."

Some of these activities could be classified as goals within themselves, or "subgoals." On a weekly or monthly basis, depending on your own ability to plan, priorities can be assigned to each goal (and each subgoal or activity, as appropriate) in order to attain or achieve the result you want.

I strongly suggest that, particularly in the case of "major" goals, or goals that require a considerable amount of planning and strategy, you set aside plateaus or accomplishment levels where you can celebrate the attaining of that subgoal. Have a party, treat yourself to something special, buy yourself a present, or do whatever you feel is appropriate to *acknowledge yourself* for having reached that particular spot in the road toward your goal.

The planning of what you do on a day-to-day, hour-by-hour, or week-by-week basis in order to achieve the results you want does not need to create confusion, uncertainty, or despair.

Your intention to realize the end result is the power that will enable you to see it happen. Your own intention is the key to having your life be the way you want it. Your intention is the power behind getting what you desire. Goals are simply a statement of what your intentions are.

How about accepting support from others? If you are totally willing to have the desired result, look at how willing you are to have other people support you in attaining it. Can you accept support? Do not ignore the reality that for a goal to be materialized, your action, your willingness to see it through, your planning and prioritizing is *vital.* It need not be an effort (in most cases, it is truly effortless) but action is needed to achieve the goal, even if it is only putting some conscious attention to it.

Remember, too, that you don't need to know how to do it—you can always get others to do it, or have them show you how to do it, teach you how to do it, etc. If a desire of yours appears foreign and outside your abilities, be willing to study and learn from people who know how to do those things; be willing to hire them or accept their advice, thus allowing them to support you in reaching your goal.

Remember that goals are anything that you want, including activities. Some activities may be planned actions that you need to do in order to achieve your main goal. Other activities may be goals of themselves. Only you can determine which activities are things you really want to do, for their own value for you, and which activities are part of your plan for accomplishing the main objective or goal.

SETTING PRIORITIES

Looking over your goals, look at each one of them and consider what priority you'll assign to it. *Subconsciously,* you will be doing this every day as you move toward your goals, but do this *consciously* at least once and notice how some of your goals have a higher desirability than others. See how some goals seem more important than others. Notice how more significance is placed on one over another.

Watch out again for the good old "I should" syndrome. It may be still lurking in the shadows and it may come back to haunt you. Don't fall into the trap of discounting your really big goals and assigning a higher priority to a less desirable, but more socially acceptable goal.

Again, be true to yourself. Maintain your integrity.

A commonly shared experience that I've heard from hundreds of people is that they are well-organized and accomplish tremendous amounts of activities, but their main objectives are not getting done! The most frequent cause of this frustration is that people preoccupy themselves with handling the lower priority tasks, activities, and goals, leaving the major goals or activities unaccomplished.

CORRECTIONS AND ADJUSTMENTS

One of the most accurate analogies I can make with respect to getting what we want is comparing our path to the path of rockets in outer space. We all acknowledge the incredible accuracy of the U. S. space ships when landing back on earth, usually within camera range of their pick-up ships, after millions of miles of space travel. These capsules are seldom on an accurate course; most of the time during their entire trip, they are *actually off course* and in the process of being corrected—perhaps as high as 98 percent of the time! In other words, while the rocket travels on a predetermined path from earth to the moon, and back, it is literally off-course most of the time!

The rocket guidance system is simply a corrective mechanism. Servo-valves, hydraulic actuators, radar sensors, and all of the other types of complicated electronic and electromechanical devices and hardware are utilized in order to make the thousands of corrections during the rocket's flight.

The analogy of the thousands of adjustments and course corrections that are made in rocket flights to our own monitoring of our personal progress toward what we want has been found to be an extremely valuable assist for people in seeing how they can correct their paths without getting stuck in personal failure—blaming themselves for being off-course.

Corrections and adjustments are not only helpful in achieving results but are *absolutely critical* in long-range goals or goals that require considerable planning.

For example, Howard and Gail have an expressed goal of owning a specific cabin cruiser, a particular model, style and color—all descriptive of being the best possible purchase to satisfy their desires at the time they set their goal. In the five years they have allotted to achieve this goal, a revolutionary new concept is developed, which totally outdates the make and model that Howard and Gail specified. If their goal was to have the best possible model available, then it might be foolish for them to continue on their path, since their ideal target has been outdated and outmoded. They need to correct their specific description to coincide with the technology that has been developed, keeping their desires aligned with the reality of the time.

How many times have you struggled and worked for something and then, after endless effort and adversity, you finally made it—you reached your goal—only to find it is not all that great?

In a seminar of about 200 people, the question was asked,

"How many of you have reached a goal and experienced it as less than satisfying?" I was surprised when more than half of those attending raised their hands—a testimonial to the necessity to keep tracking your goals.

Make sure your goals are what you still want—not what you once wanted!

At one of my first Focusing seminars, Mort shared afterward that he had realized, during the seminar, how many goals he had been carrying around as "excess baggage." These were goals that he no longer wanted, but he kept around in his head anyway, feeling guilty about having set them and not doing anything with them. The truth was—he didn't want them anymore. In the seminar, Mort realized this, which made it possible to drop them and thus free himself of all that wasted energy that he was using to carry around these old, out-of-date goals.

You do not have to know all the reasons why you are off course—JUST GET BACK ON!

A common mistake that people make in their pursuit of their goals is that they insist on "figuring out" why they are off their course.

I'm not saying that you shouldn't learn from your mistakes. Just don't get bogged down in all the reasons and explanations for why you've gone off track, or allow other things to interfere with your quest. Don't spend time feeling like a failure, blaming somebody else, seeking out reasons for why it happened, etc. Who cares? Just notice you are off course, acknowledge that this has happened, and get on with it.

Periodically, reviewing your goals list provides you with new incentive, a reminder of your targets, an opportunity to update your goals, add new goals, make corrections and adjustments as your lifestyle has moved or changed, and, generally, compare your current performance and desires with what you had previously expressed. Like Mort, you may want to drop goals you no longer desire. Your interests change all the time. Your intention may vary from one month to another, one year to the next.

IN CASE OF PROBLEMS

In the event that you sense some conflict or an exaggerated amount of difficulty in recognizing progress toward the attainment of a goal. I suggest that you take a good hard honest look, sitting down in some peaceful and serene setting, and check to see if you are really willing to have your goal as you expressed it. Just how badly do you really want it?

Is there anything that you are hanging onto that is preventing you from accomplishing, attaining, or achieving this goal? Do you have some belief or idea that you need to give up in order to see this goal realized? If you attain this goal, is any part of you, or what you identify yourself with, going to be threatened? Is there any way you'll feel "wrong" or someone else will be "right" if you manifest this desire of yours?

In one of my first Focusing seminars, a young mother shared with the group how she had just realized that she had a tendency never to complete her goals. She never allowed herself to reach the culmination of her desires. She shared with all of us that she feared that there would be nothing else to do if she accomplished her goals and, therefore, wanted them to persevere. These "incomplete goals" become thwarted intentions, however, causing her upsets and frustrations, going against her basic nature to keep moving and completing things for herself.

She feared that she might not create new goals if she completed the ones she had! She felt threatened and was hanging onto her old goals—ones that were familiar to her and that she kept around all the time.

In another Focusing seminar, Mildred, a middle-aged woman, announced that she had this feeling that she would always want more—that she'd never be totally satisfied. She was afraid that goals would never stop—that "there will always be more stuff." She was holding onto her goals and not completing them because there would just be more anyway.

So, you can see how different points of view can have the same result—in these two cases, both women quit completing/quit accomplishing for seemingly different reasons, yet very similar.

GOALS AND FUEL

Goals are like gasoline or fuel for the vehicle called "your life." If you stop supplying your life with new goals, you'll tend to drift aimlessly, starved for fuel. Some people are very content to drift, to put no conscious energy into resolving how they want things to be. They find that life works very well for them just by taking what comes. For a long time, I thought this phenomenon in some people invalidated the value of Focusing. Then, I realized that some people are content in that trust of the universe. Others, such as myself, want to see where the train is going.

It's great to have goals and get excited about what great things you are going to do. *And,* it's just as important to keep looking ahead, so you'll always have those great things to do!

In Focusing sessions, I have been constantly amazed how many people "had it made," were really cooking along in life, and then hit a period of drifting "ho-humness." They simply forgot to get gas!

They ran dry and didn't refuel. Tending your goals, maintaining and keeping them current, is just as important to a life of satisfaction as your very first list of goals.

In 1977, Dr. Peter Turla, a time-management expert, attended two of my Focusing seminars within five days. He admitted that he had not expected to gain much from the second seminar, coming so soon after the first one. However, he acknowledged uncovering many more goals for himself, even after such a short time. While he spoke, he included that three major goals had been attained, only five days after he set them!

Lloyd, a business associate of mine who also does some business consulting, was telling me that he had observed a tendency in himself regarding his business. He had observed, through his own experience, that a five to six month lag existed between the time he contacted a prospect until he received income from the client.

He also had observed that he had a tendency to back off in following up his business prospects when he was feeling "in the chips" or when he had just received payments from his clients.

As a result, he would have a definite cycle: he would develop prospects, sign up his usual percentage of them, perform his agreed-upon services, bill them, and, after five or six months, collect his fees. Then, he failed to follow up new prospects for awhile because fees were rolling in. When he noticed the fees weren't coming in as regularly, he would then put more attention on prospects, which would take another five or six months cycle, during which time he would experience some very slow months.

Like Lloyd, who needed prospects to keep income coming in down the road, we can use our clear intentions and goals as a fuel for many satisfying moments down the road.

But don't wait until you run out—keep fuel in your gas tank and you'll never run out of gas!

Don't part with your illusions. When they are gone, you may still exist, but you have ceased to live.

Mark Twain

CHAPTER XII

GOING ON FROM HERE

Now that you have this clarity as to what you want and what you don't want, what is next? Is there nothing else? Will magic make everything happen like a fairy tale?

To a very large degree, yes. If you are *willing* to have magic happen in your life, you will start to experience some miracles—magic of a unique sort as a result of having *clearly written goals.*

However, in some areas you may feel frustrated or feel a sense of conflict. These may be old barriers that you've had around for years, or new ones connected with newly discovered goals. Before going back out there in the every-day world with your goals list, give some thought to *how* you are going to get your life to be the way you want it.

ATTITUDES AND BELIEFS

Before doing anything else, check with your innerself regarding your attitudes and beliefs with respect to having all of these things you've written down. Regarding your goals, what are your beliefs and attitudes right now?

Are you willing to have them?

Do you have any beliefs that may get in the way?

Can you handle success?

Can you allow yourself to have everything *exactly* the way you want it?

Just how satisfying a life are you willing to have?

Do you believe that struggle and effort have to be involved in getting what you want? Do you believe that only unethical people can make it in business? What other attitudes and beliefs do you

BARRIERS TO OUR GOALS

have that might prevent you from experiencing a life of total satisfaction?

It's okay to acknowledge these beliefs and attitudes. We all have some. Just acknowledge them and see if they are a problem — standing in the way of getting what you want. Look and see if you have definite points of view or attitudes that may prevent you from having what you want to have. Are you holding onto positions or points-of-view that serve no purpose whatsoever, other than keeping you from having what you really want?

Decisions about money and decisions we've made about sex are the two big subjects that control us as modern 20th century humanoids. Tamara, a lovely southern California lady, had come from a home where her father and mother separated. Her father was a wealthy man and her mother apparently spent a lot of energy obtaining funds, support payments, etc., from her estranged husband. During our conversations, Tamara, who admitted to having a problem accepting an abundance of money, realized that she had made a decision about her mother, who, through her youthful eyes, was humiliating herself for money. Therefore, Tamara felt that the only way to get money was to humiliate herself, and she was unwilling to do that.

SUCCESS AND FAILURE

In a very simple form, life is a series of successes and failures. In my own opinion, there would be no purpose in our being here on earth if there were not successes or failures.

Most of us think we can identify and imagine the feeling that goes with *success.* We identify success with a good, positive feeling of accomplishment, heroes, and pioneers, "making it," the glamorous life, and, generally, the really good stuff.

However, when it comes to *failure,* most of us want to go to sleep — to hide. Many people think of a failed goal, or a failure to accomplish something, as one of the worst possible experiences they could ever endure! Our society has seemingly become more and more intolerant of failure. This popular attitude towards failure has prevented many people from ever starting anything.

Intellectually, I look upon failure, or failing to achieve a desired result, as simply that—a miss! I aimed at something and missed! Tell yourself, "I am totally willing to be responsible for the target being missed and I acknowledge myself as the cause of its being missed, but I am not going to add on a lot of judgments about my own ability or self-esteem regarding having missed it." We all tend to add on explanations, excuses, reasons, or blame to cover up the loss we feel. Notice this tendency and be prepared if it creeps into your routine.

Blame, regardless of where it is placed, serves no positive purpose. All that blame does is detract from everyone's sense of themselves, adding more fear barriers which, in turn, prevent happiness and satisfaction. Blaming yourself or others produces the same unsatisfying result.

We can recognize that failure, and the fear of it, runs a good many people. It prevents them from doing anything. It paralyzes them, in a way. An extremely valuable alteration I have made in my own attitude towards failure has been to look at failure as possible only when one quits or gives up. In other words, if I am working towards something and I have a serious setback, I can do either of two things. I can *correct* the mistake or I can *quit,* or give up. Learning from my errors and mistakes and freely choosing the next step in progressing towards my goal is not "failure" to me—it is correction, adjustment, or doing what needs to be done in order to get back on track. Remember the example of the moon rocket being off-course, perhaps as much as 98% of the time, but it still ends up right on-target.

Quitting or giving up completely is denying the possibility of ever reaching the desired result that was wanted. Now that the goal can *never* be achieved, even though it is still wanted, the condition truly becomes one of *failure.*

WALKING, AS A SUCCESS

Think of how valuable the simple act of walking is for you. Yes, just plain every-day walking! Think of the dozens or perhaps hundreds of times (as a crawling, diaper-bearing infant) that you stood on those shaky little legs and attempted your first step with or without the assistance of adults.

What if you had stopped trying to walk after the first time? What if you quit after the second time? Or the third time you attempted it?

Well, you were a failure, admit it! *Every time you failed to walk, you were a failure.* However, you endured and now enjoy the benefits of walking as you have been most of your life.

Compare this experience to situations in your life where you attempted or aimed at a goal, made a step towards a desired result, made some progress towards a personal want of yours, and stopped any future progress due to some setback, feeling like a failure. As a baby, you were willing to be a failure on numerous occasions in order to achieve the final goal, which was to walk. Evidently, you saw enough value in walking that you were motivated to continue working towards that goal.

I was using this example of persistence in a seminar when I suddenly recalled that a young woman in attendance was wearing a leg brace. Her name was Annie and I asked her to tell the group about her experience. She had been injured in a motorcycle accident and was told she'd never walk again.

While others in the room could hardly recall learning to walk, Annie provided crystal clear testimony on what it was like to learn to walk as an adult and not as a baby. She had to overcome her "adult reasonableness," the myriad of beliefs she had adapted since her youth.

If something is worth going after, it certainly is worth one or two failed steps in order to achieve the final result. Our ideas about failure, along with all the negativism we've attached to them, are what stops us—robbing us of some very valuable experiences.

OTHER EXAMPLES

A student, having a goal of getting a 97% score on a final exam in biology, for example, and actually receiving a 94%, has failed his goal. There is no question about that. That is the fact. He missed his mark.

However, the student need not consider himself "stupid—a failure," or make any other self-judgments, *unless he chooses to do so.* Other than that, it is simply a failed goal.

To those people who only have one goal in life, or maybe two, this could be really significant! To have a goal of being a millionaire means, by most people's standards, having a million dollars in net worth. Does this mean that a person who has accomplished reaching $900,000 in net worth is a failure? Hardly. It could seem so, since this individual did miss the mark, but the final attitude (the way this accomplishment is held) is up to the individual.

Be willing to make mistakes—they are bound to come up. If you fall apart or give up because you made a mistake, you'll be doomed before you begin progressing toward any personal goals for yourself. All you can do then is contract or shrink—withdrawing from life rather than expanding and participating more in it.

OUR COMFORT ZONES

Did you ever notice how people can handle only so much success? They have some idea of how much success is okay, and then there's a point to stop.

Each of us, as human beings, seems to have created a certain zone of success in which we feel comfortable. This zone we create for ourselves has limits. Below the lowest limit we feel like "failures" and we are *extremely* motivated to rise above this lowest level. Above the upper limits, we feel "too successful" or as if we are having it "too good" and we usually sabotage ourselves so we can fall back into the *comfort zone* again.

For instance, I have a dart board in my home and I have become quite proficient at dart-throwing. When I'm in very good form, I can put four or five out of the six darts into the center bullseye. Quite frequently, after throwing three or four darts into the center, I can almost hear my mind making some decision about the developing situation and, predictably, my next dart will be off-target. The thought that I see running by my internal TV screen includes the opinion or belief that it is impossible to get all six in the bullseye and, therefore, I seem to make *absolutely certain* that this belief is reinforced! In fact, sometimes I have actually *missed the board* with the next dart! My attitude (or belief) seems to be that six out of six in the bullseye is impossible and this attitude prevents me from achieving that optimum performance.

Neither reading this book nor, for that matter, writing this book, will eliminate all of these attitudes and this preconditioning. We all went through it and there's no avoiding it. All we can do is acknowledge that it exists and be aware of it, recognizing when it is running us like robots.

THE COMFORT ZONE

CELEBRATE

Acknowledge yourself when you have achieved the result that you wanted. Remember how horrible you were to yourself when you didn't attain that goal you once had? Remember how you judged and evaluated your performance and unmercifully beat yourself up about it? Well, when you've pulled off a real win— celebrate it! Treat yourself to something extremely extravagant and self-indulgent. Do something whereby you really acknowledge yourself for having achieved your win.

If it is appropriate, let others know what you've accomplished—boldly and proudly. Maybe they'll agree, maybe not. You didn't do it for them anyway, right?

SUPPORT YOURSELF

To accomplish the things you want to accomplish in your life, you need support from the universe. The first need for support comes from you, the center of your own universe.

What do you do that supports your goals and intentions? How do you live? Does your lifestyle support your getting what you want out of life? This could be a difficult question for you, so sit down and really look at how you run your life right now. Look at all the things you want—the kind of person you want to be—the things you want to do—the items you want to surround yourself with—the relationships you want to have. What are you doing to support yourself in getting this? How do you communicate? Does your vocabulary support your getting what you want? Do you speak positively and assuredly? Do you let people know what you want or do you assume that they can read your mind?

Do you use words like "try" and "hope," or do you use very positive words, indicating how strong your intentions really are? Do you use vague phrases or are you exact and precise? Do you set up appointments and other agreements so there is no doubt as to when and where things are to happen? Or do you tolerate unkept agreements and appointments?

Do you associate with people who support you and your intentions? Do your friends share your interests and goals? Do your relationships with friends and family provide support for you or could you associate with other groups who can be more supportive?

Do you live in a location that assists you in realizing your ambitions? Can you be the person you want to be in the environment in which you are presently situated? Would a different house, a different neighborhood, a different city, a different state, or country support you in attaining your goals?

Do you dress in a way that supports your purpose and intentions? Do you present yourself in a manner that reflects who you want to be? (Do you want to be recognized as being financially successful, yet you are still wearing jeans, teeshirts, and tennis shoes?)

Are your attitudes and ideas about life supporting you in accomplishing the things you want to accomplish? Do you have prejudices, beliefs, and points of view that support you? Are you willing to eliminate the ones that don't? Are you willing to learn new things in order to get what you want? Are you open to new experiences if they assist you in fulfilling your desires? Are you willing to say, "I don't know?" and ask someone else how to accomplish what you're attempting to do?

FINAL EXERCISE

I want you to do another exercise—this will be the last one in this book. I suggest you repeat it for each and every major goal you have.

For now, however, select *one* major goal. Select a goal that seems like a real challenge, where you definitely have some uncertainty about reaching it successfully.

Got one? Okay, fine.

Make absolutely certain that you *really* want it. Is it truly important to you? Really important?

Ask yourself, "About this goal, am I associated with people who support me in reaching this?"

Ask, "About this goal, am I dressing and grooming myself in a manner that supports me in attaining this for myself?"

"Am I living where I need to live to get this?"

"Am I talking and communicating as I need to talk and communicate to achieve this result?"

Ask yourself, "Do I have any notions or opinions that I need to erase or alter in order to have this thing happen?"

"Am I willing to let all my friends know that I want this thing, so that they have an opportunity to support me?"

After asking yourself all these questions, see how sure you are that you really want your goal. Is your intention still there to see this goal realized?

What else can you do to support yourself in getting this condition in your life?

If you don't know how to do all things that are necessary to get what you want, ask yourself, "Am I willing to learn how to do this?" Also, ask yourself, "Am I willing to have someone else teach me?"

If you run through this exercise with each of your "biggies," those goals to which you attach some great significance, I promise you that you will become even clearer about just how high your intention level is regarding each of them.

SUMMING UP

If you take a lesson from children, or even babies, you can see how effortless it can be to get exactly what you want. Babies have not been conditioned, as we have, and are not at all shy about expressing themselves about what they want. As a consequence, you might observe, they seem to get *precisely* what they want all the time!

Basically, all people want to contribute to their fellow man. I am not saying this from some idealistic viewpoint, or from some belief of my own. I'm reporting what I've observed. On a very basic human level, other people are not only *willing* to support us in our desires, but they are *eager* to make a contribution to our lives. *The biggest barrier we have to getting what we want is the barrier to asking for it.*

Therefore, in the form of homework, I'd like to send you on your way with Step #1 on the road to success. Verify your goals and, where it's appropriate, let others know what you want. The world will support you just as it does the infant child. *All you have to do is to know what you want and let others know that you want it.*

As kids, we had it made and we didn't even know it! We assembled all this information, while we grew into *sophisticated* adults, and we've succeeded in camouflaging our basic desires to be happy and satisfied. We have covered up our willingness to acknowledge (to ourselves and to others) what it is we have to do. All we have to do is to get our "sophisticated and conditioned minds" out of the way and it will all work perfectly!

An extremely valuable technique that can really assist you in obtaining the results that you want is the use of *affirmations,* imaging or any other form of creating more vivid representations of your written goals.

By picturing what you want, as if you already have it, the process begins whereby you naturally seem to progress towards your goals, seemingly without any effort. I use affirmations to create more positive points of view about what I want, to dissolve unwanted attitudes that seem to get in the way of progress, and to condition myself automatically to achieve goals that are representative of a continuous state, such as "being in good health."

Some examples of affirmations can be:

● "I begin each day energetically."

● "I thoroughly enjoy all of my relationships."

● "People find me to be warm and friendly."

Affirmations are positive statements to confirm that you already have a desired condition in your life. Affirmations are statements of fact about a future condition that you want. Always use the present tense when stating your affirmation. Have the subject goal stated in the desired condition, not the undesired condition (the present).

Many people who use affirmations keep them in written form and read them periodically, as often as they desire. Others, including myself, record their affirmations on audio tape and play them back at convenient times. I listen to my affirmations while driving in the car, while brushing my teeth and shaving, while dozing off at bedtime.

You may have different affirmation lists for different purposes, depending on where you want the boost. I know a dentist who has created teeth affirmations for his patients in order to have healthier mouths. I have seen affirmations to quit smoking by, lose weight by, be more successful by, and for many other self-supportive uses.

I've seen affirmations written up on index cards and posted around offices or apartments. If you have a particularly significant goal or a condition you want to have in your life, make up an affirmations sign or poster and tape it on the mirror in the bathroom, over the telephone, in the kitchen, any place where you will see it repeatedly. Affirmations work for many people—especially for those who have some personal habits that work against them.

I know some people who repeatedly write out their affirmations in long hand, each time they do the exercise. I once attended a seminar where the same affirmation was repeated, in writing, one hundred times in succession! While it may sound tedious, it forces your mind to look at that particular goal, or the barrier to the goal.

An expansion on the concept of affirmations is the idea of "imaging," physically and mentally. Envisioning what you want in such precise detail that you can see it in your mind can be extremely valuable in making progress.

Close your eyes and picture the exact condition you want to exist. Explore the situation thoroughly—check out the feeling you are experiencing. Check all your senses and savor the situation thoroughly.

This internal, very personal imaging process provides you with an experience that is as close to the real thing as you can get. It can be valuable for you if you like to keep in touch with what you are going for.

Can you remember saving up for something as a child? Can you recall your desire to see it whenever you could? If it was in a window of a department store or pictured on a page of a catalogue, you wanted to see it whenever you had the chance while you were saving your nickels and dimes.

I've seen this type of graphic affirmation hung on walls in homes, on the dashboards of cars, and made into desk-top sculptures. Within the human potential community, there are group workshops in which people get together to create their own personal posters, using the group's energy and excitement. You can really have fun with it. You can be as creative as you'd like to be. After all, it's up to you and it's your goal!

CONCLUSION

This book has been about getting clear about your intentions in life. By getting clearer, you're providing yourself with a big step towards a more fulfilling and satisfying life, no matter how fulfilling and satisfying a life you have now. This book is not a "How To Be A Success" book. However, if you want to be a *success,* and you've included the desire in your goals, and you've been explicit as to what "success" means to you, then your chances are good at getting what you want—but IT'S UP TO YOU!

This book provides you with a tool—a form with which you can look closely at yourself and determine what your intentions and desires are. But, be clear about *who* has been doing all of this. YOU HAVE. *You* have done all of the looking. *You* have done all of the listing. *You* have done all of the exercises that have brought you up to this point. None of those goals you have written down are mine. They are all *yours.* You have proceeded to this stage. From here on out, it is still *all up to you!*

What you do from here is your responsibility alone! These pages have provided you with some information and the context in which you can assess what you want in life. Through this book, I've given what I had to give. It's in your hands now.

The amount of value that you receive from this experience and the degree of responsibility you take to have your life be the way you want it depends upon your own willingness to have your life work perfectly!

ACKNOWLEDGEMENTS

I'd like to extend heartfelt thanks to all of my friends and former clients who encouraged me to complete this book, not only the writing and revising of the manuscript, but carrying it out through the printing and publishing stage. I am much more appreciative of the efforts and discipline of those who author any form of book, be it fiction or non-fiction.

Particularly, I'd like to acknowledge several of my sources for inspiration, including Abraham Maslow, Jack London, Alan Lakein, Buckminster Fuller, Paul J. Meyer and Werner Erhard.

I'd also like to thank those friends who have authored books themselves for the inspiration their accomplishments provided me, including Peter Turla, Kathleen Hawkins, Jack Reed, Jerry Richardson, Bob Larzelere and Fred Wolf.

For their direct efforts in supporting me to start, revise and finish this work, I'd like to thank Neal Rogin, Norissa Leger, Kerry Witcher, Judy Taylor, Judy Nichols, Don Sereff and Diane Behling.

Books Offered By
CONTEXT PUBLICATIONS

☐ **Winning Through Enlightenment**
by Ron Smothermon, M.D.

The principles of transformation laid bare with no extra baloney. This book, first published in 1980, has become a classic and is in its fifth printing. Over 150,000 copies sold even though it has never been advertised or promoted.

☐ **Transforming #1**   by Ron Smothermon, M.D.

After the principles of transformation are understood, what do you do with them? How do you make a difference with them? What is the opportunity in life? These areas are dealt with in masterful and entertaining detail in this ever-popular book.

☐ **The Man/Woman Book**   by Ron Smothermon, M.D.

In this book you will examine in intimate detail your relationship with all people of the opposite sex, the relationship all men and all women share with each other, and the meaning this relationship has to this time in our history. The opportunity and importance of personal and social transformation of the Man/Woman Relationship is made clear.

☐ **Playball, The Miracle of Children**
by Ron Smothermon, M.D.

Out of his own experience of his relationship with his son, Ron defines and derives a relationship with children which makes a difference. The notion that children, all children, make a profound difference, now, becomes real through this book.

☐ **The Harmony of Love**   by Bob Larzelere, M.D.

The principles of creating and maintaining love are examined in this book by a loving, mature, professional, gay man. The principles of this book hold true for people of all sexual preferences.

☐ **Setting Goals**   by John Renesch

The most simple, yet powerful means to having your life the way you want it is to master the skill of consistent setting and achieving of worthwhile goals. This book removes the mystery of how to do that.

☐ **Winning the Greatest Game of All**   by Randy Ward

Playing the multilevel marketing game so that freedom and aliveness are the result is the objective of this book. Written by a master of multilevel marketing, this book is a generic that lends itself to all multilevel marketing businesses.

☐ **Inside Out, Becoming My Own Man**   by Jed Diamond

That rarest of qualities — an author who can tell the autobiographical truth without becoming lost in egocentric details, and at the same time relate his own experience to that of the reader's experience. This book deals with one man's path to his own manhood, transcending the myths of manhood prevalent in our cultures.

☐ Diets Don't Work by Bob Schwartz

Like many areas of life, losing weight seems to make life the master, and us the mastered. Using a diet, like using any ritual, is useless, for it bypasses our natural power to exist in a natural state. Treating a condition with a ritual is making one mistake to correct another. By mastering the issue of weight, the principles of mastery become clear for all aspects of life.

☐ The Context Network, A Business of Your Own
by Ron Smothermon

If you receive value by reading and listening to the books and tapes of Context Publications and want to share it with others, this book was written for you. It outlines the business methods to create the distribution of these books and tapes as a part-time business of your own.

Audiotapes Offered By
CONTEXT PUBLICATIONS

☐ The Man/Woman Tapes by Ron Smothermon, M.D.

This series of five tapes covers some of the material offered in The Empowering Man/Woman Relationship Training. Individual tapes are on the following subjects:

MAN/WOMAN I:	HONESTY
MAN/WOMAN II:	PARENTS
MAN/WOMAN III:	SURRENDER
MAN/WOMAN IV:	COMPASSION
MAN/WOMAN V:	THE ISSUES

Musical Tapes

☐ A World That Works For Everyone by Joel Goldstein

The notion of a transformed world set to words and music by an outstanding folk singer. Moving and humorous.

☐ Amazing Grace — Flute Meditations by Michael Rose

This artist will bliss you out with his flute.

☐ Dream Maker by Noel Roth

Clear, crisp, inspiring songs of the New Age by a truly great vocalist. Including "It's In Everyone of Us."

CUMULATIVE QUANTITY DISCOUNT SCHEDULE
(OK to Mix Products for a Cumulative Discount)
PRICE PER ITEM INCLUDES SHIPPING (AND TAX WHERE APPLICABLE)

NUMBER OF ITEMS BEING ORDERED	DISCOUNT	OUT OF STATE	IN STATE	Outside U.S. must be paid by money order in U.S. dollars	
				IN CANADA IN U.S. DOLLARS	CUTSIDE U.S. AND CANADA (in U.S. Dollars)
20+	40%	$ 6.57	$ 6.93	$ 7.16	$ 7.76
10-19	30%	7.66	8.08	8.36	9.05
2-9	20%	8.76	9.23	9.55	10.35
1	0%	11.95	11.95	12.95	13.95

ORDER FORM
(PLEASE PRINT)

NAME

NUMBER   STREET   APT. NO.

CITY   STATE   ZIP

COUNTRY — IF OUTSIDE U.S.

( )   ( )
Home Phone   Work Phone

NAME OF PERSON FROM WHOM YOU LEARNED OF CONTEXT PUBLICATIONS

☐ I enclose a $ —————
  check for ————— copies

☐ Bill my VISA or MASTERCARD.
  Here is the number and expiration
  date:

  No. —————————

  Exp. Date —————————

☐ Send C.O.D. (In U.S. Only)
  (5% extra service charge + $1.95
  U.P.S. fee).
  (Applies in U.S. only)

FOR SAME DAY MAILING
VISA or MASTERCARD
ACCEPTED BY PHONE
(3% SERVICE CHARGE)
(707) 584-4423

EXAMPLE CALCULATION
FOR
10 ITEMS, OUT OF STATE:
10 + $7.66 = $76.60
THIS IS THE TOTAL COST
+ 3%
IF USING CREDIT CARD

Enclose order form with payment and mail to:
CONTEXT PUBLICATIONS
P.O. Box 2909 / Rohnert Park, CA 94928-6506, U.S.A.